UNHEARD VOICES
REFLECTIONS OF A PRISON CHAPLAIN

Imelda Wickham

Published by Messenger Publications, 2021

ISBN 9781788123365

Designed by Messenger Publications Design Department
Typeset in Adobe Caslon Pro & Sackers Open Antique
Printed by W&G Baird Ltd

Messenger Publications,
37 Leeson Place, Dublin D02 E5V0, Ireland
www.messenger.ie

CONTENTS

FOREWORD

Fr Peter McVerry

FORTY YEARS ago, I was working in the north inner city of Dublin, one of the most deprived neighbourhoods in the country, which supplied our criminal justice system with a large number of residents. St Patrick's Institution was then a juvenile detention centre for males aged sixteen to twenty-one. I knew twenty of those juveniles who were incarcerated there, all at the same time. Nineteen of them had grown up with alcoholic parents (hard drugs were not a problem at that time) and had experienced violence at the hands of those parents. Many years later, I was visiting Mountjoy Prison, where I met with nine prisoners for about an hour. Six of them had been sexually abused as children; the other three, I didn't know well enough to be able to say. I thought that if this is a reflection of the criminal justice system, what on earth are we doing? These are men who were traumatised by their childhood experiences and never received the counselling or therapy they needed. Unable to cope with the trauma, they turned to drink or drugs to escape the pain. Their addictions landed them in jail. They were victims of crime, long before they made other people victims of crime. Society, instead of helping them, once again victimised them as adults. These are the men and others like them, whose voices can be heard in Imelda Wickham's wonderful book *Unheard Voices: Reflections from a Prison Chaplain.*

Imelda was a prison chaplain for over twenty years. Prison chaplains have a unique role in the prison system. They provide pastoral care to prisoners and prison staff. Imelda explains that the role of prison chaplain gives one the freedom to be with the prisoners. She describes 'the privilege' of being able 'to walk the walk with them during their sentence'. Prison chaplains have an independence that allows them to speak the truth as they see it. Imelda has always used this independence to give prisoners a voice and this is what kept her working in a system which left her deeply troubled and still does.

In this book, Imelda humanises the often faceless, voiceless prisoner and makes visible the realities and tragic complexities of life for those in prison. Interestingly, Imelda compares walking across the threshold to join a religious order with crossing the threshold to begin prison life, but she is quick to remark that while the former is a calling and voluntary, the latter is not. Nevertheless, there are similarities: 'When one joins a religious congregation, one leaves the old life behind and *becomes* a religious. You take a vow of obedience and become subject to rules and regulations not of your own making.' This was particularly pronounced in an enclosed congregation in the days before the Second Vatican Council when Imelda took her vows and perhaps prepared her for her time behind locked gates.

Imelda raises important questions around humanity, social justice, choice, freedom, compassion, intimacy, grief, loss and human rights. She poses challenging questions about the nature of crime and punishment. She is not naïve and is very aware of the sensitivities around crime for victims and their families, but she also draws our attention to the experience of families of prisoners and the punishment they experience as loved ones of offenders. She shines a light on the everyday events of normal life – birth, death, illness – and how these have deep and significant meanings for those living apart from their loved ones. She lays bare the pain of regret, longing, helplessness, grief and loss, all exacerbated by poor literacy, isolation and long hours, days, weeks, months and years in a challenging environment.

At no point is Imelda judgemental. On the contrary, she fully acknowledges the challenges faced by those working in the prison system and recognises the great work many of them do, day after day, year in, year out, in a harsh regime and an environment which she describes as 'the labyrinth of corridors, multiple gates and doors, the vast concrete jungle that is a prison'. Imelda knows intimately the routine and language of prison life and her love of the 'wit and banter' within the prison walls is palpable and makes this book an enjoyable read. Imelda contrasts the hustle and bustle of morning routines with the poignantly described mood later in the day: 'Often in the quiet of evening time, when night was drawing near and the hidden pain was being unleashed in the silence of prison cells, people began to speak of the inner pain of separation and loss that accompany imprisonment'. It is this pain and loss that we come to understand from reading Imelda's book.

Imelda reveals a sad and disturbing picture of a dysfunctional criminal justice system, in which people are locked, for extended periods of time, in cramped prison cells. Instead of rehabilitating them, prisons often damage them further. Many of the prisoners in Irish prisons have an addiction and/or mental health problem which has never been addressed, and is unlikely to be addressed while in prison. Prison is not an environment conducive to mental health recovery. The depressing, monotonous life of prisoners can contribute to prisoners continuing to use drugs rather than helping them escape from them. Indeed, I know many young people who were first introduced to drugs while in prison. Many others are homeless; indeed, as Imelda tells us, prison, for some, has become their home, and for some becoming a prisoner makes them homeless.

Society ignores the complicated interaction of personal, familial, social, economic and political reasons why crimes are committed. Instead, the fear of crime, frequently fuelled by some politicians and some elements of the media, leads people to want a 'quick fix'. That 'quick fix' is prison. For many, the crime defines the person, and the blame for society's failures is placed entirely on the prisoners' shoulders. Many also fail to recognise that almost all prisoners will one day be released, and if they come out of prison more damaged than they went in, society becomes less safe. This is an issue that Imelda is concerned with. She is committed to promoting restorative justice. Her years working in the prison system have taught her that there must be another way: a better way of working not only with offenders but their families, their victims and the victims' families.

Imelda has done Irish society a service by shining a light on the criminal justice system. Her honest reflections come from a strong sense of the hidden potential in each prisoner and an equally strong commitment to helping to make that potential a reality. She illuminates the lack of support in an inadequately funded and staffed prison system which, despite the best efforts of some very caring staff, increasingly prioritises security over rehabilitation. While Imelda touches on very painful topics, she does it with humour and a lightness that makes her book very readable. It fills the reader with hope and a respect for the humanity of offenders and a belief that there is a better way.

INTRODUCTION

ON 3 July 2014, I received a short note from my provincial, Sister Imelda Carew, which finished with the words: 'I hope you have started writing and taking a half day every Monday for it.' This little note was a follow-up to a meeting we had the previous week where she asked me to commit to writing about my experiences as a prison chaplain.

I agreed and decided it was something I might do at some stage in the future, but for now there were no half days on a Monday or any other day for that matter. I was always too busy and had other things to attend to. Imelda used to challenge me about always being too busy and recommended that I get some balance in life, something I never got around to doing either.

However, something I did do was to keep Imelda's short note. When she and Paula Buckley died tragically in August of that same year, this little note took on a new significance. I decided that I would honour Imelda's memory by fulfilling her request to me. I was full of good intentions, but somehow I was still too busy. Maybe deep down I felt I wasn't a writer, and even if I did write, who would be bothered to read it? It wasn't that I felt I had nothing to say. I had plenty to say and still have, but committing it to paper was another thing, and, as usual, I had other things to do.

Imelda and I were good friends and shared a common passion for social justice. Imelda tended to take the long-term view. She was an advocate for addressing climate change long before it was on the national agenda. I tended to favour taking action on the here and now, addressing those issues of social injustice that affected the lives of people on a daily basis, like homelessness and the marginalisation of people being kept poor. For me there was an urgency about these matters that needed to be highlighted and brought to public attention.

Fifteen years previously I had sought and been given permission to move into prison work. I remember feeling convinced that this was what I wanted to do more than anything else in the world. It was what I had always wanted to do, and while other things took over, I never lost sight of my dream of being with people in prison. The prisoner always had a place in my heart. The little phrase in St Matthew's Gospel, 'I was in prison and you visited me', always evoked a longing in me to do just that – visit the prisoner.

I had no idea how to get into prison work, nor indeed what I would do if I got in. All I knew was that this was what I was being called to at this time in my life. I rang the governor of Mountjoy Prison. He invited me in for a day and assigned me a prison officer to show me around Mountjoy. What a day!

At the end of the day the governor asked me what I wanted to do, and I still didn't know. He advised that I go away, think about it, draw up a programme and come back with it to him. However, I was very busy at the time. I knew in my heart that this was not going to happen. He suggested I look at the prospect of becoming a prison chaplain. Even though I never had thought of that before, I decided there and then that I would begin the process of trainig to become a chaplain.

My next step was to visit Bishop Eamonn Walsh, that great friend of prisoners and prison chaplains. Eamonn encouraged me and advised me about what to do, and the rest is history. I studied counselling skills and learned about drug addiction at Loyola University in Chicago, where the social teachings of the Church came alive. I then headed for the Vanier Detention Centre in Toronto. I spent three months there in the women's prison and completed a semester in Clinical Pastoral Education. It was my first taste of prison life, and I learned a lot. I also knew that I had found my niche in life.

My abiding memory of that time is of 22 April, which is the anniversary of my profession. It is always a very special day for me, a day when I reflect on the past and think of the future. Here I was at last, after all the years of longing and waiting, in a detention centre. It was a dream come true. I had found my true vocation in life, a vocation within a vocation. I felt an overwhelming surge of gratitude.

I then began to explore the possibility of remaining in the United States as a prison chaplain. If that was the only entry point, I was prepared to uproot and move bag and baggage to the United States. What prevented me was the belief that I could better minister to my own people. I would understand my own people better and would be better able to relate to them. Life is all about relationships. With that in mind I applied for prison chaplaincy in Ireland, was successful and flew home to begin a whole new chapter of my life. I was given a five-year contract by the Archdiocese of Dublin that never ended! It was chaplaincy without parole for me!

The role of prison chaplain certainly gives one tremendous freedom to be with the prisoners and to walk the walk with them during their sentence. That was my privilege for over twenty years. During those twenty years, I met amazing people whom society had locked away out of sight. I also met some of the most disturbed and tormented individuals, many suffering from mental illness or personality disorders. I met the homeless and the addicted, the unwanted and the outcast, but I never met an evil one. People carry out evil deeds and inflict great pain and suffering on other people – at times even on themselves – but they are not evil. I have never encountered an evil person; I just met people who carried out evil deeds.

Prison is a place apart, hidden behind high walls. Barbed wire and secure gates make it difficult to get out or get in. It is a world apart where people are detained, deprived of their freedom for a period of time and become prisoners. But first and foremost, they are people, citizens of our state, members of our families and neighbourhoods. Becoming a prisoner does not change who you are. You are still the same person and worthy of dignity and respect. Becoming a prisoner is a process that begins as you are taken across the threshold of the prison institution. It continues while you struggle to bring your mind across that same threshold. This can take longer. It is the gradual realisation that the only way to survive prison is to gradually withdraw from the life you knew on the outside and become part of a new reality. This is painful. Many struggle to avoid it only to finally succumb to the inevitable. It is a survival mechanism and the only mechanism in the current prison system that enables you to survive. It is a system that needs to be renewed and reshaped to bring it into the twenty-first century, and into line with new psychological insights and new understandings of human behaviours.

This is the system that I applied to become part of, was accepted to and began to work in on 1 September 1999, the last year of the old millennium. A whole new world had opened up for me, and like the newly imprisoned crossing the prison threshold for the first time and becoming prisoners, I began the whole process of 'becoming a chaplain' in the Irish context.

Part One of this book combines my personal vocation and journey as a Presentaion Sister with my calling to prison chaplaincy. It shows how those two became one as I moved among the incarcerated and shared their lives and journeys. In Part Two I offer a series of reflections on what life can be like for people in prison.

PART ONE

CHAPTER ONE

PERSONAL CONNECTIONS

I OFTEN wonder if my desire to be with prisoners is not in some way related to my desire to enter the convent. When you join a religious congregation, you leave the old life behind and *become* a religious. You take a vow of obedience and become subject to rules and regulations not of your own making. It is not easy. It is not something I *wanted* to do but something I felt *called* to do. On a human level it was the last thing I wanted to do. I was only eighteen. I had a whole life ahead of me, and who knows what prospects! And so, it had to be a response to a higher calling. In a sense, while I was a reluctant candidate, I was convinced, and I still am, that that was what I was called to do in life. I have no regrets except to say that there is still never enough time in life to do all the things I want to do. At heart, I am still eighteen, looking out at all the possibilities life has to offer and having to choose which ones to follow!

I entered what was then an enclosed congregation. I became a virtual prisoner until the Second Vatican Council called on us to return to our founding charism and become part of the lives of the people of God, among whom we lived and worked. This I embraced with the full and total enthusiasm of the released prisoner who has served their time and has the world and freedom awaiting them. It was a good time to be alive, young and energetic. The doors were flung open and fresh air was blowing like a mighty wind among and around us.

The walls came down slowly, and new horizons beckoned. A new theology of religious life replaced the old certainties of the past. We reflected on our founding charism and realised how far we had strayed from the founding spirit. A new freedom emerged, accompanied by courageous moves to build a new way of life. This way of life, not totally embraced by all, emerged and in time the old and the new learned to live in harmony, as we tried to support and accept each other in the quest for integrity. The struggle is ongoing and contributes to keeping the energy alive as numbers dwindle. Age takes its toll on us physically, but not on our vision, our commitment, or our belief in the power of God and his care for the world.

Nothing will ever change this, even death itself. We are a joyful people struggling and living in hope by faith.

The prisoner has no such choice. His is not a free choice. The question of free choice is something I have reflected on over the years as I shared the lives and times of the people I met in prison. Their stories and mine intermingled and some common experiences, even if unspoken, emerged and opened a path of understanding and trust.

I remember when as sisters our letters, incoming and outgoing, were censored and when family visits were limited and controlled. I remember when I felt removed from family and friends, and when permission had to be sought for even the most trivial or minute issues. So, we share experiences, except for the one big difference, mine was a calling and a chosen way of life. This helped me to accept and cope with the situation. It opened doors and possibilities of a way of life that attracted me to move and work among people made poor. The tremendous freedom of religious life, when embraced to the full, is totally liberating.

On the basis of this experience, I encouraged prisoners to deal with the frustrations of prison life in the hope of a better future when they were released, when once again they would be in control of their lives and destiny. Incarceration passes for most people, and the best possible way to serve time is to use it productively. This is something extremely difficult in the current prison regime, where prisoners are locked up in cramped cell conditions for on average sixteen out of twenty-four hours, where no structured activity is provided by a service proclaiming to be a rehabilitative one. You have to be capable of self-structuring the long and tedious hours of lockup. Many are unable to do this and therein lies one of the many difficulties faced by the imprisoned.

All of us, including the incarcerated, have dreams and must aim for the realisation of our dreams. We must keep dreaming or we will imprison ourselves in the wilderness and circumstances of life. Dreams, however, can quickly turn into nightmares in the harsh and dehumanising ethos of a prison. The struggle, at times, can become too much. Escape routes are few, and where someone fails to find that route, drugs or self-harm or even suicide may seem an obvious option for the tormented soul. In this context I ask, is it not time for some prison walls to come down and for society to have the courage and foresight to explore other options to address the issues of crime and punishment?

To dare ask the question will no doubt spark off controversy. If the controversy adds to dialogue and debate, it will have been worthwhile. A fair and open debate is called for where all views – including those of people who have been in prison, their families, their victims and their victims' families – are respected and listened to. Vested interests will have to be put aside. Fresh understanding is called for and we will only fully understand when we listen with the heart as well as the head.

In the years since I became a prsion chaplain, new insights have emerged that allow for new and more creative ways of looking at crime and punishment. Crime is a complex issue. It has existed since the beginning of time. All crime causes pain and loss and damages society. The influence is far reaching. It extends beyond the immediate time and place of any particular crime. How does this happen? What role does the current system play? How we deal with perpetrators of crime will have a bearing on their future lives and careers. It will also have a bearing on the future safety and well-being of society. The time for believing that soceity is safe when the perpetrators of crime are all locked up in prison is long past. What happens in prison is crucial, and society needs to know more about it.

Life is changing, and societies worldwide are changing. Criminality is changing too, and not all crime calls for the same nature or level of punishment. This needs to be recognised and real efforts made to address the changes. What is crime? What is offending behaviour? Is there a distinction to be made between crime and offending behaviour? Only in recent decades has homosexuality been decriminalised. Maybe there are other areas we need to examine. Maybe the time has come to decriminalise drug addiction and see it instead as a medical matter.

Addictions are multifaceted and the addict does not choose his or her addiction. Victims of addiction will suffer lifelong pain and trauma that may last for generations. Untreated addictions have cast dark shadows over this country, shadows that will continue to lengthen if perpetrators are not treated and victims protected. Locking the addict in prison where minimal treatment is provided will not protect the innocent. We also need to question the appropriateness of a prison setting. It is time we looked to establishing treatment centres with fully qualified staff for those suffering from addiction. We should leave prisons for those who absolutely require it.

CHAPTER TWO

INTRODUCTION TO PRISON LIFE

MY FIRST few years in prison gave me an insight into the lives of the people I met with on a daily basis and into what life within the prison walls was like for the men committed there by the courts. I also observed what it was like for staff and prison management. I had a lot to learn, but I found many willing teachers, not least among the prison population who recognised the greenhorn and volunteered to help me find my way around the labyrinth of corridors, multiple gates and doors, the vast concrete jungle that is a prison. I appreciated the help, and they enjoyed being of help. We soon got to know each other, and each morning the new arrivals were introduced to me by the more mature members of the establishment. I felt totally at home and knew instinctively that this was where I belonged. I felt no fear and experienced no intimidation. I just felt totally accepted and soon got to know the morning routine of the prison. It was explained to me that if there was toilet paper draped over the handle of a cell door that meant that someone was using the toilet. Nobody would enter the cell during that time. This was useful information, and we all respected the little niceties that were expected of us.

The mornings began for me on the drag,[1] where it seemed the whole prison population was emerging from cells all at the same time. There were men everywhere, going to school, going to workshops, going to the yards or wherever. It was a bit like the M50 but maybe not as slow. Everyone was on the move, except for the men on lockup, and over the years I must have walked thousands of miles. Yes I walked the walk, the same walk every day for twenty years and got nowhere, just ending up where I began all the time. Wherever the Spirit led me I went, and I always depended on the Spirit to bring me to where I was most needed. Insofar as I know, the Spirit never let me down.

Early morning was a good time for a chaplain to be out and about. It was a time to meet and greet. At this early hour, I was always fascinated

---

[1] Main corridor.

15

by the good humour of everyone. How could someone emerge from a prison cell, having been locked up for on average 13 hours, with a smile and a greeting? And the wit! I enjoyed the wit and the banter. This created a normality that was anything but normal, but it kept us going. In my heart I often thanked God for the 'messer', as we called the guy who had the ability to make us laugh, even when life was anything but a laugh. Deep down I knew that the wit and banter was a survival mechanism, a cover for what was going on inside. I have no doubt that they also knew this. There are few survival mechanisms in prison, and you have to learn which ones to use and when.

As time went on I learned to look out for the troubled and anxious ones, and make sure that we met later in the day, or at evening time, to have the chat and see what was going on for them. It was during these times that the harsh reality of prison life would emerge and untold stories of times past would finally be told. Often in the quiet of evening time, when night was drawing near and the hidden pain was being unleashed in the silence of prison cells, people began to speak of the inner pain of separation and loss that accompany imprisonment. Keeping the best side out is a daily requirement in prison. It is not good or indeed acceptable to be seen to be vulnerable or weak while serving time in prison. It can in fact lead to other challenges or difficulties. 'Do your whack'[2] is the mantra. Few meaningful relationships are formed in prison. It is the survival of the fittest. The thin line between friend and foe can snap in an instant.

I have also found pockets of real empathy and concern among the men, especially among those serving long sentences. I remember times when I had to break devastatingly sad news to a prisoner. While I would be carrying out that hard task, the men on the landing would keep at a good distance to give us space and privacy. After I had left, they would slowly move into the cell. They would offer to make a cuppa and share a few roll ups with the bereaved. They would offer their own experiences of grief. I always appreciated this, knowing that when I was gone there were others there who cared and were willing to offer support. I knew too that they would speak a common language and share an experience that I didn't have.

I learned a lot from these encounters and marvelled at the tremendous ability of the men to cope with such tragedies and grief, separated

---

[2] Prison sentence.

from those close to them. For the most part they were not allowed attend funerals. Some were allowed view the remains in funeral homes accompanied by prison staff and then return to prison. The men always told me that the hardest thing of all about being in prison was getting bad news, and for me the hardest thing that I had to do was to break bad news to them. And when the men would thank me for coming to them, I felt so humbled, that in all their grief and loss they wanted to say thanks. It was at times like this that I questioned a system that can find no other name for these men except criminals. They are human beings, just like the rest of us.

The hidden pain of separation from family and friends, and especially separation from children, is one that causes the most severe suffering. The enforced celibacy imposed on the imprisoned has consequences rarely recognised by society. The denial of human intimacy is akin to a type of physical and emotional death. People who choose celibacy, as I did, do so for a reason or a cause and it is rooted in a way of life or a calling. It is chosen and embraced on a voluntary basis. Forced celibacy is another issue, and while I am not suggesting that it be removed, I am asking that it be recognised and taken into account as part of the imposed punishment.

If we say imprisonment is about rehabilitation, we need to look at the environment in which we place people and the added deprivations that are imposed on top of the loss of liberty. We need to recognise the emotional and sensory deprivation that results when contact with family and friends is confined to visists that are structured and monitored by the prison, and where concrete and steel replace green spaces and blue skies. These deprivations affect the psychological well-being and physical health of the imprisoned in unseen but worrying ways.

The more I walked among the imprisoned, the more I came to realise the enormity of their sentences. It was not just the length of time imposed by the judges; it was more about what happened to them while time was being served that troubled me. The high rate of recidivism in prisons is generally accepted as being what it is, with no real effort being made to analyse the why. Recidivism cannot be viewed in isolation. It is closely linked with the whole issue of the harmful effects of imprisonment and the very real damage incarceration does to people, a damage that affects them for life, and makes the return to the outside difficult to negotiate. The stigma of imprisonment is not left at the prison gate. It continues to follow you. The accompanying rejection can make life so difficult, that life on the inside seems preferable to life on the outside. Some prisoners are unconsciously drawn back in.

Anyone who crosses the threshold of a prison will be adversely affected. The length of the sentence and the age at which you enter the criminal justice system both have a bearing on the extent of the damage. Imprisonment does not just deprive people of their freedom, it de-skills and de-socialises them. It takes away their decision-making capacity and it lowers their self-esteem, while depriving them of the ability to earn a living or to support a family. All of this could be avoided if punishment did not figure so high on the scale of priorities. Punishment extends far beyond the perpetrator of the crime; it affects whole families and causes untold intergenerational damage. From my experience, leaving prison for many was as stressful as coming in, and many expressed very real fear and anxiety at the prospect.

The rate of homelessness among the prison population is high. Many enter the criminal justice system as a result of being homeless; others become homeless as a result of imprisonment. The difficulty of maintaining family relationships is a contributory factor. To avoid being classified as 'no fixed address' on the prison committal form, many will use a false address. The current housing problem makes it twice as difficult for the homeless leaving prison, so homelessness is another contributory factor to the high level of recidivism. Prison becomes home and home becomes prison.

CHAPTER THREE

ORDINARY PEOPLE

ANY ONE day can bring a variety of emotions to the surface as you walk the walk and talk the talk in a prison environment, and this was my experience as I trudged the highways and byways of the prison. The men used to ask me now and again how long I had done this, and commented on my answer by shaking their heads and saying, 'Worse than any life sentence without parole Imelda.' Many serving life began the same year as I did, and we had a special bond. I got to know them, their families, their backgrounds, their histories and their aspirations. Their crime didn't define who they were, and I had to frequently remind them of this. Many of the imprisoned are made to feel that they are their crime and no longer enjoy that common privilege of being a unique individual deserving of human dignity and respect, with the same feelings and aspirations common to all of us. Keeping that sense of who you are is so important for all of us. It is especially important when one is feeling useless, worthless and being called 'a scumbag'.

Some might think that people in prison don't aspire to achieve, but they do. To achieve their aspirations, however, will often feel like climbing mountains, only to be pushed back down, while all the time the mountain seems to be getting steeper and higher. This is the direct result of inadequate resources and the indirect result of poor educational background combined with poor self-image and lack of confidence. Those who persevere and attain even the smallest of successes are filled with justifiable pride, and so begins a journey that can lead to a whole new way of being. My greatest joy was to see people grow in self-awareness and self-esteem. To see the joy of a man celebrating even a small achievement was my joy.

Those returning to the outside will be burdened by the stigma of imprisonment, and it will require extraordinary courage and effort to overcome. Many do, and I have the greatest admiration for them. I also totally understand those who find it too difficult. Sometimes life just becomes too hard and the burden too heavy. In the effort, many lose heart and hope, and succumb to drugs as a way to deal with the frustrations and barriers. The role of the chaplain is to support and sustain them in this journey. I remember at times feeling that I was the one climbing the mountain, as door after door was closed in the face of someone I was journeying with. So, all we could do was to keep on the journey together and live each day in prison as we would live it on the outside.

It is important to develop skills and strategies to deal with life in prison. One strategy is to see the events of life on the inside as mirroring life on the outside. Life on the outside can seem rosy and easy compared to the one on the inside, and some reminders are needed that this is not the case. Prison isn't the only depriver of freedom; many on the outside have their mountains to climb. Their courage and example can often be the inspiration those on the inside need to keep going. The efforts made by staff and management are not to be ignored either. They try, within the limitation of the system, to help the people committed to their care. Dealing with the system can be the hardest thing of all.

I have written elsewhere about the harmful effects of imprisonment and, while not wanting to hurt anyone or be too judgemental, I will add the following observation. Imprisonment can make you selfish, and I can understand why. Left with nothing and nobody, you can easily turn in on yourself and develop a 'poor me' attitude. The effort to cope with the harshness of prison life and the recurring memories of happier times can lead to the illusion that on the outside all is well and all manner of things are well. Not so!

At times it seemed to me that minds were paralysed or frozen in time, and an inability to let go of the past and live in the present prevented the men from making progress. While life on the outside was changing, and people were changing and moving on, men on the inside were waiting just to return to what they had left behind without appreciating that there was no going back. All will have changed, and they too will have changed. This is not easy to accept, but is part of the reality of life. A good rehabilitation programme, if one existed, could address this issue. It could help prepare all involved prepare a reintegration process.

Prison can also bring out the very best in people, and I witnessed the most extraordinary generosity at times. A memory that remains with me, and that had a lasting effect on me, is that of a young man who was due to be released from prison. He was homeless, and it troubled me to think that the following day, the day of his release, he would be alone with nobody and have nothing. Things would be worse for him on the outside. I made my way down to see him armed with a few Players Blue and not sure what I was going to say to him. At least he would have a smoke the next day. His cell mate was out when I arrived, and as we chatted, I advised that he hide the few Players Blue for himself, so that he would have a smoke when he got out. Ever so nicely he told me that he always shared what he had with his cell mate! This lesson I learned over and over again, and I often wondered who was ministering to whom.

I came to realise that the families of people in prison were also serving a sentence. Young mothers left to rear the family, earn a living and maintain a home, if they had one, were serving a sentence. Elderly parents struggling to visit an erring child were serving a sentence. Indeed all who shared the consequences of imprisonment, were also serving a sentence. It is a recognised fact that children of incarcerated parents are more likely than their peers to end up in prison. I believe that these matters need to be kept in mind when addressing the issue of crime and punishment. This is part of a conversation that needs to take place when looking at alternatives to imprisonment.

Many of the incarcerated worry so much about family on the outside that they are unable to do time productively. This can lead to depression and high levels of anxiety that in turn is transmitted to family members. Embracing life's circumstances helps us live life to the full and prepare for a future that is ours alone. There is life after prison, and the best way to prepare for it is to live life to the very best of our ability while serving time.

Those who survive prison by living well on the inside will survive life on the outside, because they have continued to live life to the full on the inside. Those who refuse to fully live while inside will find it difficult to survive on the outside. It is a question of attitude, an attitude that has to be learned and embraced. This is a challenge that demands discipline and maturity. You have to learn how to cope with the constant battle to keep in the right frame of mind, but it is a battle worth fighting.

These are some of the issues that we shared and talked about as we sat in prison cells or corners of workshops or classrooms, anywhere we found a safe and quiet place to have a chat. We didn't need interviewing rooms or offices. As chaplains, we had access to all parts of the prison and enjoyed the freedom of the children of God and the Prison Service! This facilitated all of us in using every possible opportunity available to us to get to know the men and the staff, and for them to get to know us.

When I first began working in the prison, chaplains did not carry keys and we depended on the goodwill of officers to let us through gates and doors *ad infinitum*. This they always did with graciousness and good humour, and together we worked to make the prison as good a place as we could within the rules and regulations. I think too that we succeeded most of the time. We all worked within the same system and the various and multiple limitations imposed on each of us in accordance with the role we played within it. Where respect for that role was the underlying principle, it worked well.

There is something special about the prison community because that is what it is, a community. At times it may not have felt that way to all, but deep down that sense of community prevailed, and we tried to live together as best we could. Confined spaces, frayed nerves and past histories all conspired to make life difficult for all at times, but we still managed to live together. Sunday mornings were special. It was the morning when we came together to pray. It didn't matter that some didn't join us, because those who did represented the whole body. We prayed for the sick, the dead and the dying. We prayed for new babies and remembered birthdays and anniversaries. The names of people and their needs were called out, and we all answered 'Lord, graciously hear us.' And He did. We prayed too for those who would be leaving us during the coming week and for those who would be joining us. Mothers and fathers, brothers and sisters were all remembered. It was a good place to be, and if at times our rituals were not entirely according to Roman Rituals, for us, they were sufficient. It is the same Lord who is over all. Ritual, after all, is meant to reflect life, and our Sunday liturgies reflected life as we lived it.

CHAPTER FOUR

'SHOULD I STAY OR SHOULD I GO?'

THE CHAPLAIN holds a unique place within the prison and is chaplain to the entire prison community. Their calling is threefold. Firstly, they are to be people of faith, exercising a prophetic role in their stance for justice. Secondly, they are called to be a voice for those deprived of their freedom. Thirdly, they are called to promote the principles and practices of restorative justice, and to be a healing link with the wider community. It is a Gospel-based calling and has the authority of the Gospel, and thereby places a certain responsibility on the shoulders of the chaplain to be faithful to their calling and to exercise it within the parameters of prison rules and regulations. I stayed in response to that calling. I stayed because it was my way of being with people on the margins, and nobody is closer to the margins than those in our prisons.

In my role as chaplain I had free access to all parts of the prison outside of lockup times. This gave me the freedom and opportunity to be with the men as their needs emerged. It was in these encounters that life stories were told and retold. It was from these encounters that subsequent contact was made with families. Within a short time it became obvious that many of the men suffered from multiple losses in their lives, so we set up a bereavement support group, where facilitators were invited to come in on a weekly basis and run support meetings. While dealing with loss and grief, many of us will seek the support of family and friends and some will seek professional help. People in prison may find no such outlets. Sometimes their grief is compounded by guilt and regret, and without the possibility of help the only way to cope is to bury feelings. Buried feelings, however, don't go away and will emerge in different negative forms as life progresses. The men embraced the opportunity to attend the support group and often spoke of the freeing experience of unburdening themselves and of helping others in the group to do the same. Men who participated in these groups witnessed something unique in the daily life of imprisonment. They learned the lessons of self and peer support that carried them forward and created a special bond among them, based on mutual trust and confidentiality. Strict confidentiality was central to the success of the group, and was respected by all, at all times. That this could happen in a prison environment was most encouraging, and it showed the ability of the men to engage in a meaningful way once the atmosphere and environment was right. The initiative was fully supported by prison management and staff.

This was followed by the setting up of an introduction to mindfulness course, and such was the demand that the course was regularly oversubscribed. Not only did the facilitator come in on a weekly basis, but at one stage he was joined by three young students from Trinity College. They came not to teach but as equals, to practice together the art of mindfulness. I am not sure who benefitted the most, but it was a wonderful coming together of people from different walks of life and different backgrounds, with a common purpose, in a non-judgemental setting.

During this time it became obvious that we needed a sacred space within the prison. Somewhere all would be welcome to 'come apart and rest' (Mk 6:30–34). We met with prison management and plans were discussed. Eventually a place was decided on and best of all, the work was to be carried out by officers from the workshops with some of the men who were being trained there. It was a great experience for all involved, and they took a well-deserved pride in completing it. It is called The Sanctuary and is just that, a place apart. It is a haven of peace and holds within its walls the *prie-dieu*[3] specially made for Pope Francis when he visited Ireland in 2018. His anticipated visit to a prison didn't take place, but we were ready, just in case! It was made in the joinery workshop and taken out to the Papal Nuncio's residence. It was blessed by Pope Francis during his stay there and then taken back to the prison and placed in The Sanctuary.

Contact with the outside world contributes greatly to the life of a prison, and as chaplains we appreciate the openness and welcome extended to visitors by prison management. Choirs came to help with our Sunday liturgy and our own special prison choir, when we had one, would join them. Our choir was known to rise and fall in membership, depending on the comings and goings of the prison population. On joining the choir, I would ask the men how long they had left. When their time was almost finished, they would smile as I asked them to extend their stay a little longer just to help us on Sunday mornings!

---

[3] A form of prayer desk.

Some beautiful musicians and singers joined us on occasions too, and added to the life of the prison in such a beautiful way. Choir practices were joyful, happy occasions. Not all those who joined the choir could sing. It wasn't a pre-requisite. I remember a last-minute practice one Christmas, where only one of the seven who attended could sing, and he was due to be released on Christmas Eve! We had, however, some wonderful talent. I can still hear the strains of 'The Lonely Boatman' played on the tin whistle. We had some amazing guitarists and wonderful singers. We would build up a great choir, and then they would leave us, and we had to start all over again.

The first Christmas I spent in the prison, I was contacted by a group of young students. They offered to come in on Christmas morning to sing and play Christmas carols for us. We welcomed them with open arms. For years afterwards they never missed a Christmas, until one by one they began to move on. Finally we were left with just two. They got married and are still coming, not just for Christmas but as often as they can. These great people became part of the prison community, and we loved to see them coming.

The visits and the visitors were like shining lights coming among us, and I have no doubt that they took something precious away with them when they left. People in prison develop a wisdom of their own. It is a wisdom not enjoyed by those who have never experienced the depth of loneliness of the prisoner. For many, who have endured long court sessions, sentencing and unrelenting media coverage, prison is almost a welcome respite. I have vivid memories of petrified men fearing a frenzied attack following a newspaper article written by a journalist who had never met them or knew them. The simple truth that, in spite of what he is guilty of, a man is more than his crime is one of the hardest of lessons to convey. It is a long process to help individuals to believe that, first of all for the offender and secondly for the wider community.

I had a special interest in people coming into prison for the first time. I watched with dismay as they were gradually assimilated into prison life. It was the beginning of what would be a lifelong pattern for some of them. That the state was prepared to pay thousands of taxpayers' hard-earned money was baffling. Who conceived of the idea that locking people up is the answer to offending or criminal behaviour? Did anyone ever ask why so many of our prison population have spent almost their entire life locked away? Judges sentence the same people over and over again; the prison system houses them over and over again; the same media who demonise them and report on them to a couldn't-care-less society report on the same people over and over again, and prison chaplains work with the same people over and over again. Yet we all fail to ask the question, 'Why?'

As the years passed, and as I advanced in age if not in wisdom, I began to notice the numbers coming into prison who were homeless on entry. I also noticed that many who came with an address were leaving without one. Homelessness and imprisonment are closely linked. While there is some sympathy for the homeless person, there is little for the homeless prisoner who struggles to pick up the pieces of life on release. The stigma of imprisonment casts long and lasting shadows, and makes life doubly difficult for the returning citizen.

As a society, while we are prepared to spend on average €75,000 a year to keep a person in prison, we are then prepared to hand them a see-through plastic bag for their scant possessions, a bus pass, if needed, and a certificate of imprisonment on release. Is this a return to freedom or another bind? For those lucky to have some place to go, this may be of some help, for the homeless it is a temporary pass to nowhere. This is a social issue that is being ignored. As I watched what was happening, it became impossible to just watch. Something had to be done, and I lacked the skill and expertise to do it. I knew, however, that others possessed what I lacked, and so I set about meeting them.

What I found was an ocean of goodwill, knowledge, experience, generosity and willingness. I was overwhelmed by the response of people who gave of their time to help their fellow citizens on the margins. No research was needed, we knew the needs, and so we became an action group. As a result an organisation called TRAIL (Transitional Residential Accommodation for Independent Living) was established, with the initial primary funding coming from religious congregations committed to social justice. This was later augmented by capital assistance grants for the purchase of accommodation and so began a story of what can be achieved when action in response to need is taken.

The aim was simply to address the complex needs of homeless people leaving prison and to also offer an opportunity to those seeking to make a fresh start in life following incarceration. Integration was central to our ethos, and with this in mind, people were offered an average of six months transitional time in private apartments scattered throughout the city of

Dublin and its environs. Support staff was available to help them make a seamless transition from custody to the community. It worked, and today people look to TRAIL as a way out of the binding bond of imprisonment and homelessness towards a way of life that recognises the potential of each one to become the person they were meant to be.

The emphasis is on the future potential of the person rather than on past failings. It was truly counter-cultural at the time and became a small beacon of hope in the otherwise darkness of re-integration. The hope was that the model would be replicated to ensure that all would be offered a place. To date this has not happened, and so the cycle continues. The initiative did create a new energy among the men as they worked towards achieving a place with TRAIL. There was, however, an underling issue that failed to go away, namely the harmful effects of imprisonment. The more this became obvious the more the words of T. K. Whitaker rang true. Prison should only be used 'as a measure of last resort'.

CHAPTER FIVE

PRISON AS A LAST RESORT

PEOPLE SERVING life sentences do on average seventeen years in prison. Some serve many more years before being released on licence. I have walked the long road to freedom with this special cohort of people, towards the exit, as freedom beckoned. I have met them on the outside as they have tried to negotiate their re-integration into a sometimes unwelcoming and uncaring society. Best of all, I have celebrated with them their successful re-entry.

Some people, though never given life sentences, nevertheless, serve life incrementally. They are often referred to as repeat offenders, recidivists or career criminals, by people with little knowledge of the criminal justice system, and by people who rarely ask 'Why?' Why do they keep coming back to prison? Is life easier on the inside or are they merely law breakers? In the eyes of the world they are the authors of their own destiny and become virtual outcasts often even from their own kith and kin.

As a chaplain, I have sat with them, listened to them and tried to understand them. Their stories have a common thread running through them. Yet, each story has its own uniqueness. Each story is a deeply personal one told in the first person. There is some sadness in the listening. Each story carries within it unheard evidence of guilt or innocence, evidence not required by the courts of law, evidence not of public importance and therefore not of interest to the media. But, this unheard evidence carries within it a depth of truth that is crying out to be heard.

The stories and the storytellers are banished from our midst to where they will serve time and pay back their debt to society. What happens seems of little concern to the public. Yet it is the public who will pay for their keep while they are held in the safe and secure custody of the state, unable to make any meaningful contribution to society or any meaningful reparation to the people damaged by their actions. That there may be other ways of paying back the debt is seldom discussed.

Imprisonment in Ireland is intergenerational. Many of the imprisoned have experienced prison prior to their own conviction. As children they visited their fathers or other close relatives in prison, sometimes for many years. Prison became part of their everyday lives. Fathers returning into their lives at varying intervals often led to family upheaval and confused emotions; love, hatred, admiration, shame, guilt, all intertwined into childhood years, only to be followed by the next disappearance and the next weekly trudging to prison. It was all the same. Sometimes the effort to cope became too much and the only escape route was drugs, drink or simply to follow in the footsteps of the one who went before. And so the cycle continues from one generation to the next. This cycle needs to be broken.

Like society on the outside, life on the inside has its own social structures. Some come into prison on a once-off basis and tend to come from better off homes, have a fairly regular standard of education and have some work experience. From their life experiences, and encouraged by parents, they will avail of the opportunities afforded them in the prison. They will attend school or workshops on a regular basis and avail of any extra-curricular activities offered to them. They will have accommodation on release and are unlikely to return to prison. They will have paid their debt to society, if that is how it has to be paid, but in the process will have been damaged by the experience. They will carry the stigma of imprisonment with them for the rest of their lives, and the memory of the experience will be imbedded forever in their psyche.

There is another group who are regular visitors and have grown old in the art of doing time. They have learned how to do time and feel at home when they arrive. The staff know them and will look after them. I remember a young man who had entered the justice system at a young age. He explained how he found it so difficult to survive on the outside that he deliberately committed another crime in order to get back in. He described the prison officer taking him down to his cell and pointing out his bunk to him. 'I threw in my bedding,' he said, 'and then threw myself onto the bunk bed and felt at home.'

Then there is the final group: the young and uninitiated, who are beginning a life on the inside. Many come from broken homes or from 'no home' situations. Some come from care institutions or from youth detention centres. Many come from the streets, but all come carrying within them the youthful fear of the unknown, combined with the naive anticipation of what may lie ahead. I look at them and wonder 'what has been' while knowing 'what will be' for the vast majority of them. They are entering a drug-infested zone that no young person should ever have to enter. What brought them here, will keep them here. They have crossed a threshold of no return. I have met them in their coming and in their going. I have watched them rise and fall. I have struggled with them, fought with them, chided them and loved them. I have pleaded with them and for them. We have become like family.

There must be other ways of dealing more effectively with the issue of crime and punishment, other interventions that would bring about a reduction in crime as opposed to its increase; a way that would bring healing and restoration to victims and perpetrators of crime, and ultimately a way that would lead to a restoration of right relationships between them in the form of a restorative justice model.

If imprisonment should be a last resort, surely it is no longer acceptable that we confine people to prisons without ensuring that while in custody there is an emphasis on personal development, education and training suitable to the needs of each one. Prisons need to be equipped and staffed to provide the rehabilitative needs of the person in their care. This would necessitate an increase in the number of prison personnel, counsellors/psychologists and other professionals allocated to each institution. This would require a parallel of commitment from prisoners to avail of the help offered to them. Incentives for the completion of required programmes would give hope to the incarcerated, develop their self-esteem and prepare them for a structured return to normal life.

Prisons could become places of human development and places of education and training. They could become places where wrong doing is admitted and addressed and where preparation for re-entry into society becomes the focus and direction of a rehabilitative programme. Coupled with this approach must be the education of society in how to welcome back the one who has strayed from the social, cultural and moral norms required of all citizens in civilised societies. Demonising and stigmatising has never worked. It merely leads to further alienation and isolation, where the only response left to the returning member of the community is to return to the old ways.

I remember sitting with a young man who had been released as he tried to give expression to what it was like for him. 'I just can't manage it,' he said, referring to his new found freedom. 'I don't want to go back to the old way but it is all I know, so I feel caught in the middle.' He came back in, went into a deep depression for some time, recovered from it and settled into prison life. The net result of it all was that another victim was added to our statistics.

It has to be asked, is it beyond the bounds of the imagination for the imprisoned to be afforded an opportunity to earn a living while incarcerated? Would it be wrong for them to support themselves and their families? Could this be a way for them to make restitution? It is beyond time to reduce the vast numbers entering our prisons at enormous expense to the exchequer and to explore more effective alternatives.

Society at large needs to refocus attention on crime and stop believing that locking people up creates safer communities. Prisons will always be needed for small cohorts of people, but are not needed for the vast numbers currently imprisoned. Let's explore the alternatives for them. The current reality for the vast numbers entering the prison system is that they will never be able to access services appropriate to their needs, simply because there are never enough services to respond to the large numbers being committed by the courts. This is unjust and unfair. The frustration and helplessness of prisoners who seek help and fail to get it is worrying. It breeds negativity and undermines the goodwill of staff and service providers. Without adequate services rehabilitation is not possible.

CHAPTER SIX

PRISON CHANGED ME

I HAVE been changed over the past twenty years; this is what prison did to me, and for me. My beliefs and old certainties have been challenged beyond measure. I am no longer as sure about things as I was before I set out on my journey as a prison chaplain. I am still being slowly changed.

During those years I have accompanied so many people deemed unfit to remain in mainstream society. While accompanying them, I was also being accompanied by them. It was a two-way street, and I always knew that either of us could just as easily have been on the opposite side given different life experiences and circumstances.

That great divide between good and evil, them and us, slowly began to fade. The exhortation to love the sinner while hating the sin began to sink in, and the old divides became blurred. My language began to change, and I spoke of people instead of prisoners. Sex offenders became people who had sexually offended. Prisoners' families became families of people in prison. We are all people created in the same image and likeness, worthy of our dignity and the respect of others. We are all on the same journey of life, with its ups and downs, strengths and weaknesses, and all in need of redemption.

With time I learned the gift and value of patience, and the need we all have to be given the second or maybe the third or even fourth chance. Change is slow and for some very slow. There may even be times when change is beyond our capacity, or the opportunities for change never come our way. During my formative years in the prison, I learned something of the fragility of our human nature. I also learned something of the resilience of human nature, and I marvelled, at times, at just how resilient it is. I marvelled too at the courage of those who failed over and over again but who never gave up, especially those suffering from addictions.

Addiction is one of the great diseases of our day, and to be so afflicted is to be condemned to a life long struggle. People who are addicts populate our prisons in huge numbers. Prisons are not treatment centres and are not meant to be. Addiction is a medical issue requiring treatment.

If treatment centres were provided for those suffering from addictions, whether the addiction be drugs, drink, sex or gambling, our prison population would fall, and our prisons would then be enabled to deal appropriately with those convicted of criminality. Currently, our prisons are called upon not just to care for people convicted of serious crimes but also people who are mentally ill and who suffer from addiction. In many instances the only place a homeless person can call home is a prison cell.

During my work, I watched the slow and gradual destruction of human lives, blighted by drug addiction. In desperation, I sought answers but found none. I observed the daily supply of methadone and people waiting patiently for their daily fix to survive yet another day's craving. To me this was merely substituting one drug for another. Some called it maintenance. I saw it as holding the addicted person in the grip of addiction and failing to address either the addiction itself or more importantly the underlying causes of the addiction. Addiction is a craving or a longing for relief; it is a cry to be responded to.

Prison chaplains have repeatedly asked that people suffering from addictions be offered treatment in fully equipped treatment centres and not in prisons. Addiction is not a crime. It is a health issue that needs to be attended to medically and psychologically. That this fell on deaf ears is not the fault of the prison system but rather a lack of political will on the part of successive governments, who use our prison institutions as care centres for the addict and the mentally ill. This is why the prison population continues to grow and expand, and prisons are unable to fulfil their true role in society. The issue of drugs and addiction is a complex one, but the complexity should not deter the people with ultimate responsibility from seeking appropriate solutions. The current so-called solutions are not working.

For many, drug addiction is associated with poverty, homelessness and crime, and the association is a valid one. People in dire poverty will seek ways of coping to deaden its pain. Those coping with the rejection of homelessness, while experiencing the daily and nightly grind of finding safe shelter from cold and hunger, will also seek relief; a relief in many instances offered by willing, unscrupulous drug suppliers who build their lucrative empire on the backs of the poor. The devious, criminal paths of the major drug dealers wind their ways through the highways and byways of the poor, the prisoner and the tormented addict while carefully avoiding and escaping the forces of the law. They wind their way into our penal institutions on the back of these same people who carry not just the burden of a prison sentence but also major drug debts, which will have to be paid in full either by the debtor or their family. And so the cycle continues from one generation to the next, never to be broken. Vested interests are protected, wittingly or unwittingly, while we continue to paper over the cracks.

I have also observed how the addicted poor are criminalised, while addicted celebrities are fêted and celebrated. Let's not ignore this fact and add further to the hypocrisy we have come to accept. The consumption and widespread use of recreational drugs at dinner parties is no less criminal than their use among the poor who populate our streets, prisons, homeless hostels and poverty-stricken neighbourhoods. While the death of any one person is a tragedy to be mourned, the death of the street addict is viewed by many in a very different light to the death of the celebrity. This is wrong.

Another aspect that struck me during this time were the hidden gifts and skills of people in the prison system. Many were totally unaware of these talents until, often, with the encouragement of a teacher or prison officer, the unknown treasure within them was drawn forth. Great artistic skills emerged, and many in the workshops developed industrial skills that led to job opportunities hitherto unknown or unavailable to them. The hidden gifts, skills and talents led them to a new self-confidence and a new belief in themselves.

For a short period during my time there, our prison population included seventeen-year-old children. I was probably seen as the granny figure to this young cohort, and I must admit I had a very soft spot for them. Some of them came from the care system and carried within their very psyche the hurt of rejection inflicted on them at an early age. No amount of 'grannying' would ever make up for this loss, but we tried. The prison was ill-equipped to cater for the needs of these children, and staff had no special training to care for them. The efforts, made by so many people over the years, to make it illegal to hold children in an adult prison eventually bore fruit. One by one the children left, only for many of them to return to us again as young adults. They returned to another of the state's penal institutions, thereby proving, that imprisoning the young does not work. Neither does it deter them from crime. Often a life of crime begins in the very place where we put young vulnerable first timers. When will we learn? Do we want to learn?

At times I became impatient with the amount of research being carried out on prisons and people in prison, crime and punishment, youth justice, I could go on. The reality on the ground gave some credence to the findings of this research. Nonetheless, little change, if any, resulted from it. The researchers seldom, if ever, invited the people most affected by imprisonment to participate in the research, or to give their views. We talked about them but not to them. In the process they became statistics rather than people. 'Come and see' became a mantra for me, and I yearned to issue an open invitation to all interested or uninterested to come and see how their hard-earned money was being used. I yearned for someone to research the outcomes of imprisonment, even from an economic point of view, outcomes not just for society at large but also for those confined. I yearned to invite in the judges who impose sentences without ever fully appreciating what they were sentencing people to. I longed for the researchers to follow through on their work and see if it made any difference. I longed for some real response to the issues identified in the findings.

I was most changed by the people who visited the prison on a weekly basis, some for many, many years. 'I was in prison and you visited me' (Mt 25:36) came alive for me. These people were living the Gospel and giving expression to the call of the Gospel in a real and meaningful way. The one thing prisoners long for is a visit; that human contact that says 'You are worth it, we love you, we miss you, we still care for you and will always be there for you.' The rejection felt by those who never get a visit must be the hardest thing of all to bear. Can you imagine what it must be like to never get a visit or even a Christmas card? And there is no one you can put on your phone card. There are such people. And when they die, if they die in prison, there will be nobody to mourn their loss. 'Alone with none but thee my God, I journey on my way' is a prayer from the Divine Office that I pray on a regular basis. I have learned to pray it for those who are truly alone – the forgotten incarcerated. Only they can pray that prayer in sincerity and truth.

In all my years I never met an evil person. People do evil things and we are all capable of that. I don't condone evil deeds, and when they occur the perpetrator must be called to justice and make amends. We all need the protection of the law to make us feel safe, and the law must be invoked when it is broken. How it responds, however, is something that needs to be examined. In traditional Christian teaching, St Thomas

Aquinas and other scholastic philosophers said that people normally do not consciously choose evil, but they choose something that *appears good* inside of their framework. I am no scholar of scholastic philosophy, but I learned the truth of this as I walked the highways and byways of the prison. And as I learned, I came to realise the futility of our response to criminal behaviour.

Being in prison is to be at the edges; it is to be set apart, away from, isolated and marginalised. To be there with those on the edges is a blessing and a grace. I discovered among them my own vulnerability and my weaknesses. They showed me who I was and challenged my deep-seated arrogance and ignorance. The two-way street merged into one-way and ultimately we all travelled in the same direction, carrying our baggage. At times we helped each other unload the baggage of the past and prepare to walk free and unfettered into a future, hitherto unknown to our deeper selves.

Breaking down walls and barriers is called for. Prejudices and false assumptions need to be challenged. People guilty of crimes also need to be challenged and take responsibility for their actions. Locking them up in prisons, where all meaningful responsibility is taken away and survival becomes the primary focus, is not the way to do this. For some, prison has become a way of life or a second home. This also needs to be challenged. If the same person continued to enter a hospital with the same condition, be treated and sent out only to return again and again, questions would be asked and answers called for. But when this occurs in the criminal justice system, no questions are asked or answers called for. The returning person is named as a recidivist and all the responsibility laid on their shoulders. And while they need to take responsibility, so do many others including society at large.

We are told that the only person we can change is ourselves, and that is true, but systems can only be changed by people. Systems can fossilise and defenders of systems can over time become part of them. This was a danger that I tried to avoid. We are all capable of getting used to the way things are and the way they have always been done. For that reason I came to value time out where I could simply think and reflect. I also learned to value studying whatever research was being carried out on our behalf. But, the greatest learning was to be in touch with the experience of the people I was sent to serve. Listening to them surpassed all the research in the world. They were the experts, but nobody was listening to them.

I also learned to value contact with the families of people in prison. They carry a burden and serve a sentence not of their making. For some it is a life-long sentence as imprisonment is often intergenerational. For others, it may be a new experience carrying with it public humiliation and stigmatisation. For many it is like a family bereavement, which can last for years. For all it is an unwanted intrusion into everyday life that will be embraced or ignored.

CHAPTER SEVEN

FAMILIES

FAMILIES OF people in prison are among the most forgotten in our society. They are the unseen, secondary or tertiary victims of crime who will carry an undeserved shame and humiliation because of the deeds of a family member. They may be innocent, but they will carry the burden of guilt by association that society imposes on them, and that many of us, knowingly or unknowingly, willingly or unwillingly, impose on them. This is their lot, and little or no support is available to them. Many go behind closed doors and exclude themselves from social contact as a way of coping. Others accept the challenge and adapt to a new way of living. It may be living as a single parent while the other parent serves their time, or looking after grandchildren while a son or daughter serves time. For many parents it may mean watching a young son or daughter go down the path of crime and enter the criminal justice system where imprisonment will become a way of life. These parents will come to know years of unending pain and anguish, while they watch one of their very own succumb to a way of life they were never meant for. They will experience the helplessness of being mere bystanders unable to stem a tide of relentless waywardness. For all affected by imprisonment, life will change.

One of the most abiding memories of my time in prison is seeing the constant stream of family members entering the prison gates, at that point where the long walk to the prison entrance begins. From there on it is a series of queues. If they arrive early, the first queue will be outside the waiting room, waiting for the door to be opened at the appointed time. The atmosphere and comfort inside will be a welcome respite for the weary and tired but, before they can enjoy it, they must queue again to book the visit. The cuppa and brief rest provided at this stage help prepare them for yet another queue, where they will go through airport-like security that includes sniffer dogs. And on it goes, through doors, gates and checks.

As I watched this process through the years, I decided that these people were the unrecognised saints of our time and the unsung heroes of family life. Here, in this hidden place of punishment, the unconditional love of God himself was being played out day by day, week by week and year by year. Here in this place of punishment, true and vibrant Christianity was being lived unseen and unnoticed. 'I was in prison and you visited me' (Mt 25:36).

The constant stream of visitors included babies in buggies being pushed in to see fathers or mothers, brothers or sisters, and members of extended families. First communicants and the recently confirmed in the faith, all came in their sacramental finery to see and to be seen. What memories these young people must carry of their big day. The old and infirm came too, some with that look of resignation or desperation that says, 'when will all of this be over?' Visiting prisons has been part of their lives for years. They know the routine, they know the staff and they know how it all works. They also know that this is a prison and that you abide by the rules of the institution at all times. The family has to learn how to negotiate the routine so that they will see the loved one on the inside. This is all that matters. They are loyal, selfless and faithful to the end.

The weekly visit to the prison, for some, was like an extension of family life. I remember a mother telling me how when her firstborn, then eighteen years old, got into trouble for the first time she had other children to look after, and she worked full-time. She decided, however, that he needed to know that he belonged to a family, and his younger siblings needed to know that he was their brother. For years she never missed a weekly visit, always accompanied by one or two of his brothers and sisters. She never complained; he was her son, and she was his mother. What greater pain than for a mother to see her child imprisoned?

Those who visit and those visited form a kind of secure unit and create family bonds that transcend the great divide that separates the imprisoned from the outside world. On the inside, however, where that great divide is never crossed, there remains the poorest of all people; those whom nobody visits. There are some who never get a card or letter and never make a phone call because there is nobody to call. This must be the ultimate in human rejection. I was in prison and you never came to visit me. This must be the loneliest place on earth. It is a vacuum that can only be filled by prison staff or other services within the prison system and indeed by fellow inmates. Many staff members and fellow inmates fill this gap, and I can only say well done to each and every one of them.

Human relationships are complex and fragile, and imprisonment can wreck the fragility where it exists. This in turn leads to an inhumanity unknown to those of us who have never experienced this kind of total isolation and aloneness. I marvel at the strength of the men to survive this and, in my own times of quiet withdrawal and reflection, I remember them in their aloneness. I remember too their estranged family members and recognise their pain and suffering. With time I came to understand those who didn't or couldn't visit. The great chasm that divided them carried within its depths the pain and suffering of a separation that could never be filled or healed.

The greatest single gift we can bring to a prison is a touch of humanity, and that small touch may go a long way towards easing a rising tension or healing bruised feelings. I remember how, before the advent of computerised visits, an elderly prison officer in charge of family visits used to call out to me each morning, as I crossed the prison yard on my way in, 'Any requests today sister?' This was to ensure that if someone needed a little extra time they would be given it. They might have travelled a long way to visit the prison, experienced a recent bereavement or simply carried an extra burden. That officer will never know how many lives he touched or how many families he helped in the course of his duties as a prison officer. Frontline staff play a vital role in our prisons, and many do a wonderful job.

During my time working in the prison I was, for the most part, occupied and concerned for the imprisoned, and regretted the little time I could spend with their families. But, they were always there in the background of my mind. Their phone calls to the chaplains' office were a daily occurrence, and sometimes were a lifeline that helped maintain broken relationships or keep the flow of information moving between them. We welcomed these phone calls, and telephone relationships very often developed between the chaplain and significant family members, and over time we got to know each other. Through it all, I learned the importance of human contact and the vital role it plays among a prison population and their families.

The calls I remember best are the ones made or received on the morning following someone's first day in prison. The fear of the unknown for the one inside and the worry and anxiety of the one on the outside were palpable, but were usually alleviated following assurances by the chaplain that all was well. This began a relationship that could endure for years. If those phones could speak, they would throw light on the plight of the families of people in prison. The struggle of these families needs to be acknowledged, respected and responded to. Families need to be given a voice in the criminal justice system. For everyone we commit to prison, there is an innocent family affected.

CHAPTER EIGHT

PRISON IN A PANDEMIC

DESPITE THE experience of working in the prison for many years, I don't believe I ever fully appreciated the enormous effect being locked up for so many hours a day would have on people. It was the way things were. It was the daily regime in all prisons, and we all accepted it as normal practice. The prisoner accepted it too. Then Covid-19 descended upon us and with it the experience of lockdown, self-isolation and cocooning. We struggled with the demands made on us, but complied with the rules in the interest of public safety. It was difficult and, as time went on, restrictions began to take their toll. Fears began to emerge that this new regime was adversely affecting our mental health. Children's social and educational development were being jeopardised, young people were experiencing high levels of stress and anxiety, and many of the elderly were experiencing devastating loneliness and in some cases, even a sense of abandonment.

As I listened to the daily moans and groans, and at times made my own mournful contribution to the conversations, I remembered the prisoners. I noticed that nobody was talking about them. Maybe no one knew that they were isolated for many hours each day. Stuck in prison cells the size of the average bathroom alone or with two or three others. And, if no one knew, why didn't they know? Maybe nobody wanted to know. And if they did know, would they be concerned about the adverse effects of this on the people so confined? If lockdown was affecting us and our mental health, would it not also affect them? These questions trouble me.

My own experience of cocooning has given me a renewed sense of what it must be like to be cocooned in a prison cell for hours that melt into days, weeks, months and years. Maybe when Covid-19 lessens its grip on us and, as a people, we begin to reflect on our own experiences and how it affected us, we may spare a thought for those whose lives are in the control of a criminal justice system that imposes its own relentless lockdown on them. As human beings, regardless of what they may have done, prisoners are no different to us. The fact that many of them entered the criminal justice system already suffering serious mental health problems should alert us to the dangers the system further imposes on them.

Their need to make reparation and restitution, and society's right to demand that they accept responsibility, is unchanged. How we approach this, however, is what is important. I am reminded of Winston Churchill's famous statement, 'the mood and temper of the public in regard to the treatment of crime and criminals is one of the most unfailing tests of the civilisation of any country'. My hope is that Covid-19 will have softened the current public mood and temper of this small nation when it comes to addressing the issue of crime and punishment. I hope people realise that crime and punishment can be addressed in a humane and restorative way.

It is to be hoped that the dual effects of isolation and increased lock–up times on the men and women in our care will be recognised and responded to in a meaningful and practical way. Covid-19 has taken its toll on society at large and on the more vulnerable, including the imprisoned, in particular. This must be acknowledged and addressed.

CHAPTER NINE

WE NEED A CONVERSATION

WHEN SISTER Imelda Carew asked me to write about my experience of working as a prison chaplain, we didn't discuss what aspects of chaplaincy I would write about. When I eventually got down to writing, what came to me was not chaplaincy but the men I had lived and worked among for twenty years. Their voices are seldom, if ever, heard, and it is their voices that need to be heard and listened to. It would be presumptuous of me to think that I can speak for them. I have never stood in their shoes or lived their experiences. I was encouraged, however, by the opportunity Imelda had offered me to be a voice for those deprived of a voice. I would not speak for them, but I would show something of what their lives were like.

Our prisons, like our hospitals and schools, are state institutions and are part and parcel of the fabric of society. However, unlike other state institutions, they are hidden from public view. Even those who visit are confined to visiting areas, and only those who work or live there have access to the inner regions of these public institutions.

My hope is to play a role in starting a conversation and dialogue on the whole issue of crime and punishment, imprisonment and responsibility. We need an open and honest conversation where all are invited to the table, a conversation that will free us to explore new and radical ways of addressing emerging issues. This is not the time for apportioning blame or passing judgement. There is no time for such luxury. What is called for is openness and honesty; what is called for is the ability to seek the truth having explored the facts, asked the questions and analysed the answers. The ability to do this can be cultivated if we all join the conversation as equals. It is not a tabloid-sensationalist approach or a listening-to-the-experts approach. We all need to have a say, including the experts, and underpinning our input must be the belief in the basic innate goodness of people coupled with the recognition of the fragility and weaknesses of human nature. This is not to deny the presence of evil among us. It is how we deal with evil that matters. We can come up with ways of dealing with evil that preserve our sense of the innate goodness of people and protects the well-being of society.

We need a new direction to take us into the future, where we can explore the reasons behind crime and examine how we address the causes. The complexity of the causes should not deter us in our quest or force us to stop the conversation. No, we stay with the reasons and listen, especially to the victims and the perpetrators. We hold the pain of both and in that holding we learn something of the deep suffering of both. And as we learn, we suspend judgement and seek rather to understand.

Dialogue and debates currently take place on time-limited television programmes, where participants vie with each other to prove their point of view or win the argument. The issues get clouded or lost in point scoring and sound bites that leave the public more confused than ever.

Prisons are closed institutions concealed behind high walls, gates, doors and barbed wire. They are not open to the outside world, and what goes on there is never seen or experienced by anyone except prison staff and the people sent there from our criminal courts. Visits by outside agencies, such as personnel from the headquarters of the Irish Prison Service or the inspectors of prisons, are occasional. What they see and witness is limited by the very nature of an occasional visit. The great work that is carried out on a daily basis by local prison management and staff is never witnessed by members of the public. Neither are the failures of the system witnessed or challenged. Closed institutions are by their very nature, just that, closed institutions, carrying within them all the inherent dangers of such.

We must, of course, appreciate and respect the need for the privacy of the imprisoned, a privacy that they have a right to. But maybe if there was a greater acceptance and understanding of the reasons why people end up in prison, privacy issues could and would be overcome. The physical barriers erected between the outside world and the world of the imprisoned create psychological and fear-laden barriers, which create the myth that prisons are dangerous places inhabited only by dangerous people and punitive staff. Nothing can be further from the truth. Prison populations reflect societal populations where the good and not so good struggle to live and let live, with an emphasis on the struggle. We need to keep in mind too that not all the not-so-good people are imprisoned.

Prisons need to be seen as places where people, experiencing certain difficulties in life, are being helped and re-trained for their future involvement in society. Public perceptions need to be challenged. People who populate our prisons are members of our families, our extended families, neighbourhoods, towns, cities and villages. Given a different set of circumstances or situations it could be you or me, my mother or father, brother or sister, son or daughter who make up the prison population.

People come to prison from all walks of life. The small numbers classified as white-collar criminals have broadened the socio-economic base of the population somewhat, but not significantly enough to bring about any major change. The vast majority of the prison population still comes from marginalised and disadvantaged areas. Deprivation, poverty, neglect and abuse ensure that people on the margins are caught in the web of exclusion from the day they are born. For some, prison may be the only stability they will ever know, and life after prison will simply mean a return to the old ways and the old places. This is accepted but ignored by a society grown used to imprisoning the poor without ever fully reflecting on the consequences. As human beings we are all capable of human error, and often it is our circumstances in life, limited educational opportunities or sheer bad luck, that lead us to crime. Prisons need to be seen in a new light and our imprisoned as members of a wider human family of life deserving of our understanding and respect.

During my time as prison chaplain I often found it strange that we bring people into custody and hold them there at great financial cost to the state, while claiming to be rehabilitating them for their return to society. The reality is that it is not possible to prepare someone for a future way of life while you deprive them of the means of experiencing what this way of life is going to entail for them. Life is about making choices and decisions; it is about taking responsibility for ourselves; it is about earning a just living and contributing to the good of society. While in prison these responsibilities and many more are taken from you, and you are subjected to a way of life that will never adequately prepare you for life on the outside. Whatever skills you had prior to imprisonment are soon diminished as your every move is dictated and directed by institutional rules and regulations.

In additiont to stripping people of all responsibility, imprisonment also strips people of their social skills. From the time you enter a prison you will no longer sit at a table to have a meal with friends or family; you will no longer form a meaningful social relationship with others. Rather you will discover ways and means of staying safe and avoiding in-prison conflicts and disputes. You will learn, if you are wise, to deal with your frustrations and walk away when tempted to lash out. Any work skills you may have acquired on the outside will, for the most part, be lost. Out-of-cell time of about seven hours daily will seriously affect your skill level unless you are one of the lucky ones who gain access to workshops. The workshops are the lifeline of the few who are able to access them when they are open, but staff shortgaes can seriously limit access.

Some of the best workshops in the state are in our prisons, due to the insight and dedication of some of the enlightened prison governors who saw the value and rehabilitative nature of work. Sadly, the actual work, while providing training and upskilling, is limited by social mores that say prisoners are not allowed make a living or support themselves or their families while serving time. They learn how to build a wall or design a fireplace, and when completed it will be knocked down to create space for the next person to learn the skill. I have seen such talent being wasted within prisons. Prisons could facilitate small industries where people could earn a living, pay for their keep and support a family. This would make not just good financial and economic sense, but also good social and moral sense. It would also give a sense of purpose in life to the incarcerated, as opposed to the long years of idleness and purposeless living that many experience in our penal institutions.

Others, lucky enough to find their way to the education unit, may discover hidden talents and skills they never knew they possessed. Here a whole new world of learning and knowledge will open up for them, and they will experience a social interaction with teachers and other staff members who will play a key role in their otherwise bleak lives. However, many who qualify and are suitable for further education or work will be denied opportunities to attend interviews for required assessments. It is difficult to keep motivated in these circumstances, some do and some don't. There is little incentive to keep going in this situation.

Another alternative is the exercise yard, beloved by some but feared by most. Many people will spend years in prison and never go to a yard, and one can only imagine the effect this must have on their physical, psychological and mental well-being. Prison life is not easy. Maybe it is not meant to be but if, as is claimed, it is ultimately meant to prepare people for re-entry into society, it is failing miserably; and failing in spite of all the best efforts of prison staff and others who work there.

Maybe if media outlets took greater care to accurately report prison conditions, the general public would be better served. During my years as a chaplain, I have witnessed new and creative measures by the Irish Prison

Service to help those in their care take steps to facilitate an easier return to society and then witnessed the withdrawal of such steps in response to media reporting and public interventions. Frequently media reporting is inaccurate and misleading and arouses public fears and protests. I would appeal to the media to get facts right not just in the interest of the people in prison but also in the interest of victims. The public has a right to know the truth.

In June 2019, media reports that people serving life sentences could be released after serving just seven years were totally inaccurate. At that time prisoners who had served seven years of a life sentence were met and interviewed by the parole board but never released. There is a long and detailed process to be embraced by people serving life sentences before being released on license. A life sentence is a life sentence, but people may be released after an average of seventeen years to continue that sentence in the community on license and under the control and supervision of the probation service. Any breach of the law will result in their immediate return to custody.

During the past twenty years, I have watched the coming and going of so many only to see them repeat that coming and going over and over again. In my frustration I judged them and wondered when would they 'get sense', only to eventually realise that it was not the *comers and goers* who lacked sense, and my frustration moved from them to a system that made it impossible for them to succeed in making the transition from prison to life on the outside. In fact, I believe that the system is a major contributing factor to the high rate of recidivism among the prison population, with second place being given to sections of an uncaring and small-minded society, whose attitude is to lock people up and throw away the key.

A conversation is not about blaming or looking for scapegoats. It is simply to express views and listen to the views of others. It is to listen with the heart and the head to all who sit at the table and not just to the voices that express views similar to our own. This conversation will explore new, creative and just ways of dealing with crime and punishment. It will explore a more holistic approach that will minimise the terrible effects of imprisonment on the incarcerated, on their families, especially children, and on the victims of crime. Central to the story must be the men and women who are incarcerated within prison walls, some for many, many years. And central too must be the victims of crime; victims who suffer life-changing trauma with no possibility of redress, except a court decision that aims to give the expression of justice being done. Victims and perpetrators are intrinsically linked, but linked destructively by the current criminal justice system. This needs to change and change radically. Change calls for courage, radical change calls for radical courage. Where will it be found? We cannot continue to pay lip service to an unworkable system, and we do so at a cost to society and to future generations of our citizens.

PART TWO

INTRODUCTION

ALONE AND IN ISOLATION

I HAVE always been fascinated by monasteries and contemplative convents, where men and women spend long periods of time in isolation and silence. In the hush and bustle of my own life, I often envied them and longed for the tranquillity and peace that seemed to emanate from the very walls surrounding them. As I walked within the prison walls and walked among the people held on lockup and in isolation, I rarely experienced that sense of tranquillity and peace emanating from prison cells. I did, however, experience some inexplicable thing emanating from the men living there. What was it? I am still not sure.

A small cohort of our people in prison spend long hours, days, weeks, months and even years in enforced silence. They are alone with little or no human contact, except with prison staff or management. I struggled to understand how they coped. What were the long days and nights alone like for them? For some, the heightened awareness of their situation must have drained all hope from their tormented minds. For others, the guilt and shame of what brought them there must have enveloped their very souls. And there was nobody there to talk to – no easing of the pain except the onset of numbness.

What sustained them? What inner strength did they possess? What resilience? Was it a learned resilience from childhood abuse? Or from extreme poverty? Or from social exclusion? I have never sat in that cell abandoned and alone as they did. I just visited them, always ill at ease in their presence. The image of their isolated figures has never left me, and I ask myself was it enough to have just visited them? I still see them in my mind's eye. I wonder where they are and how they are. Are they still alone?

Even as I ask this question, I realise that ultimately we are all alone in life. There is a depth to our being where no other being can enter. Sometimes I may be unable to enter myself. It is that deep calling on deep – my very soul, the soul of my being.

I remember the prisoner, the prisoner in the crowded prison, yet alone in heart and mind. He is among his fellow human beings who have been outcast by society., yet he is alone. No different from the rest of us, he will integrate where he finds himself and become part of the status quo. But, in the depths of his being he will know an aloneness reserved for the prisoner, reserved for the one who has lost all else. Deprived of all trappings and faced with his own naked vulnerability, he will enter a depth many of us will never enter and find there a wisdom that will sustain him. Cast afloat on the waters of aloneness, he can enter the depths and find himself, or find the struggle too much and miss the opportunity.

The following reflections give some insight into the deep emotional turmoil faced by people affected by imprisonment. They aim to give expression to the sense of isolation and aloneness; the sense of regret, shame, fear and in some cases sheer desperation of people affected by imprisonment. Each relection is offered as a means of awakening a response in us and to help us connect with the hidden voices and the unspoken pain of the incarcerated and their families. The reflections collectively give witnesss to the courage and strength of the human spirit. The collective voices merge into one thereby telling the story of all.

The Waiting Room

TWO MOTHERS sit in silence side by side in the prison waiting room. Both carry a burden too heavy to share.

A number is called. An old man rises painfully, collects his visiting pass and shuffles towards the door. It is the first of many doors and gates he will shuffle through before he sits with his son on his weekly visits to the prison, a visit he lives for.

The two mothers remain in silence. It is mostly silent in prison visiting rooms. Sometimes the silence is broken by questioning children or crying babies. But, there is little communication.

The two mothers wait. Their numbers have not yet been called. They sit locked in the silent grief of mothers whose sons are serving life sentences. They stare ahead, perplexed. They will never understand.

A number is called. A mother rises, collects her visiting pass and heads for the familiar route, out the door, across the yard, in the next door, through the gate, across another yard, another door and then just one more door left. He is waiting for her under the watchful eyes of prison staff and security cameras.

They greet each other awkwardly but lovingly, mother and son. The unbreakable bond of birth, of life, of love.

Mother, behold your son.

Son, behold your mother.

Behold Love.

Back in the waiting room another number is called. Another woman rises and crosses the yard, silently, with heavy steps and grieving heart.

As evening falls the visiting room empties. Another silence descends. A silent emptiness which carries in its very soul the sighs and sorrows of mothers and fathers, the cries of little children and the lonely passions of young lovers.

Even In Death

THE HEARSE makes its way towards the church followed by a group of ten. Sisters, a niece, a nephew or two, her partner of thirty years, a few neighbours who remember her and finally her only son and child. She is welcomed at the church door, and the coffin is wheeled up the aisle. A few symbols of her tragic life are silently handed to the priest. The readings, the Word of God, are read to the small congregation. 'There are many rooms in my Father's house' (Jn 14:2). There was little room for her in life and even less for her son, who felt abandoned by her and spent most of his troubled life in prison.

The responsorial psalm – 'Fresh and green are the pastures where he gives me repose'. Fresh and green? Rotten and bleak more likely. His mind wanders as the Word of God is read. He is back in the children's home and in the various foster homes he was sent to. Children's homes, foster homes, what the hell is a home? Prison was home for many years. It is all a jumble in his head. People are saying they are sorry. Sorry for what? That she abandoned him? Sorry for him? He is not looking for pity. He feels only numbness.

The small group begins to move. The coffin is raised. The son struggles to re-enter the scene. He steps forward and helps carry her coffin, his mother's coffin. His mother? She carried him in her womb for nine months and then forgot him? Maybe? Maybe not? He will never know.

When He Is Ready

SHE ATTENDED the court case. She saw him being taken away for life. That is the last time she saw him. She still loved him, and he loved her. But, meeting? No, that would be too much, too much for her and for him. Maybe someday, but not just yet.

She carried an old photograph of him as a handsome young fellow with his carefree life ahead of him. All has changed, but not her love for him. It will endure forever. His siblings will never understand this. He brought disgrace on her and on them. He has changed their lives forever. They have blotted him out. It is easier for them to cope this way.

Recently she spoke to him on the phone for the first time. She filled him in about his father and told him little bits and pieces of news until the six minutes were up. He moved away to make room for the next man waiting for the phone. In the silence and peace of his cell he just sat motionless, overwhelmed with shock. He heard her voice again. They spoke. There was no rancour or anger. They just spoke. He was shaking.

The abrupt ending of the phone call left his mother holding a silent mouthpiece. It is over, the six minute conversation, the first in countless years. But, she heard his voice. They spoke. They will talk again, she tells herself, and next time she will have other little bits and pieces to tell him. She will be ready the next time.

A ray of hope swelled within her. Someday they will meet. They will embrace and cry and hug, someday. When he is ready. She will wait until then.

I'm In Prison When He Is Out

SHE STILL believes she loves him but not enough to want him out of prison. 'When he's out, I'm in prison,' she says. For years she has known nothing but fear and intimidation when he is around. In the beginning she paid bail to keep him out of prison and now blames herself for being so stupid. But as she says 'you do your best'. She carries a weight of guilt, shame and blame on her shoulders, and hopes that someday maybe she will find some reason to be proud of him. He is still her son, and she wonders where she went wrong.

The neighbours are good to her, but she is still the mother of the local criminal. Nobody would want him back in the neighbourhood any more than herself. Still, wouldn't it be nice to have your son call to see you and maybe bring the grandchildren now and again, the normal kind of thing? But somehow that won't happen now, and the fear would still be there. It is the crippling fear that still grips her. She is afraid not to be afraid. If she lost the fear and he came out, and she let him back in and it all began again. NO! Let the fear be a reminder to her that nothing has changed. Still she wonders maybe someday? She will write the letter and slip in the few euro for his smokes. She knows he is safe inside. They are both safe now.

The Post Office

SHE TRAVELS across the city to post the tracksuit and runners to her son. Nobody knows he is in prison, not even her sister. She keeps to herself and has no friends, just acquaintances. It is best that way. Her son is abroad, working. He rings her every night. He has his own family now and it is not easy to get home. That is enough information for her nosy neighbours. Yes, he rings every night from prison and yes, it is not easy to get home and yes, he has his own family now, prisoners and staff of the prison.

Sending off the little bits and pieces makes her feel better. It gives her a purpose in life. She will look after him as long as she is able. There is nobody else, just the two of them, Well, not really the two of them – just her and him, two separate people, two separate lives.

The Grave

HE SEES the chaplain coming towards his cell. He senses something. Is it his mother? She is old now and he worries he will not get out before she dies. He feels the panic rise. It is not his mother. It is his young daughter. He screams and bangs the cell walls. Screams become sobs. The helpless sobs of a broken father who wails for his child.

There is no comfort. No easing of pain. Encaged in the walls of his prison cell, alone he is comfortless. He will never see her again or hear her voice or feel her love. She is gone. Her grave will be there when he gets out, and he will visit it and bring flowers. Her grave, like his prison cell – dark, cold, loveless.

The Happiest Man In The World

EVERYBODY LOVES him, but he doesn't love himself. He is kind and funny and loves attention. The attention seeking is a mask that suddenly erupts into uncontrollable sobs of pain. It is just the pain that he is carrying. There is no respite from it. He will never be able to forgive himself. He mourns his lost family. He never deserved them. They never deserved him.

Healing comes from an encounter where grace is offered and embraced. He feels a surge of love and of being loved. It is enough. For now he is the happiest man in the world.

Where Do I Belong?

I SIT with him in the café. He has just been released again. Things are not working out well for him and he is angry and defensive. In between the anger and defence, we try but fail to connect. Suddenly he asks: 'Where do I belong?' He goes silent and ponders his own unanswered question. All his questioning leads to more and more questions, but never to an answer.

'Why am I still here?' He wonders. There must be a reason he is still here. What is it?

As if drifting in and out of presence or consciousness he tries to focus. Drugged, his eyes close and open. His speech is slurred. He is trying to make sense, not just of life, but of himself.

Next week he will see what he can do. His mobile rings again. This time it seems urgent. 'I will,' he responds to the caller. 'Will meet you in about five minutes.'

He is gone.

Life Means Life

HE RECEIVED a life sentence when he was just eighteen years old. He has spent more than half of his life in prison. He was released on a number of occasions on licence and for various reasons ended back up in the system. At this stage he wondered if it was worth trying again. Drink, homelessness, loneliness, social exclusion; all played a part in his failure to cope. Each time he returned with less and less confidence in himself and in his sense of his own unique identity.

The various services had offered solutions and he accepted them. They knew what he needed to do or did they? He tried to abide by conditions and regulations. He accepted the supports, but they were not the supports he needed. He learned not to trust. He learned that life on the outside was harder than life on the inside. He gave up trying and went back in again, this time for good. To cope with his sense of failure, he turned to drugs. He is now dependent on a *legalised drug*. Is this all we can offer him?

Maybe he was listened to but not heard. Maybe we listened but didn't hear.

The System Is The Punishment

HE HAS just been told that his son has been involved in an accident. He is in ICU suffering multiple and serious injuries. He is shocked and numb at the same time. He has just a few weeks left to serve, but knows he is unlikely to be given early release. Imprisonment is no problem to him. He has previously explained to me that he copes by just being numb. 'Numb' is a favourite word of his. He also talks of fear. He fears he won't cope when he gets out and wonders if he should go to a treatment centre again, if they will take him. It would be a sort of refuge for him.

In his state of shock, he begins to talk about his son and their difficult relationship. He speaks of the love he has for him and how he would try to explain things to him on his release. His son has his own issues to deal with, and he hopes his son will not end up like his old dad.

He fears getting out and fears not getting out.

His seriously injured son is constantly before him.

He wants to get out. He doesn't want to get out.

The system won't allow him out to see his seriously injured son.

There Is Only Me

HE GETS two visits a week from his partner, and he rings her every day. But now there is no answer when he rings. Visiting times come and go, and he is not called. He is worried. He panics. Every day and every effort brings the same response of no response. He sends for the chaplain. Her efforts fail too. She enquires if she might ring someone else; someone who might know where his partner is and if she is ok. But, there is no one else. 'There is only me,' he says, 'Maybe she has dumped me.'

A little further exploration reveals that she has been getting her daily methadone in one of the city's clinics. Slowly the realisation that, yes, she has dumped him, sinks in.

He is in prison. 'I was in prison and you visited me.' He is in prison and his partner used to visit him, but not anymore. He walks away humiliated and alone. He walks into his cell where his mate is going on about, on about, oh what is he on about? Oh, if only he could be alone, alone. Darkness and despair. Rejected and dejected. Alone in mind and heart, amid the chatter and indifference of all around him. There is no escape from the inner turmoil that fills him and the routine turmoil of the cramped cell and noisy prison landing. Does anyone care?

He's The Only One I Have

IT IS late in the prison. It is 7.20pm! Time for lockup. The day is almost over, and everyone is heading for the cell. 'Bang them out there now lads,' is to be heard as officers do their last round of the day and secure the cell doors for the night. The long fourteen-hour night begins.

News has just come to the prison that his father is in intensive care and is not expected to recover. It is late, but it is decided that it is important that he is told. The chaplain makes her way to his cell. Officers stand outside the door while the news is broken to him.

He is distraught and pleads to be taken to see his father. We tell him we will try to get him to the hospital in the morning. Looking at us with fearful and frightened eyes he asks, 'But what if he dies tonight? He is the only one I have.' We have no answer. It is late in the prison. It is 7.30pm!

We leave. We leave the frightened teenager alone. The door is locked; locked for the next thirteen hours. What if his father, the only one he has, dies tonight? I return shortly to the locked cell and push some tobacco under the door. I look in. He is lying across the bed.

In a desperate effort to offer some small comfort, I tell him I will light three candles when I go home, one for him, one for his little sister, and one for his Da, *the only one he has.*

The Photographs

SHE REMEMBERS the day he made his First Holy Communion, and the day he made his Confirmation, and the day he passed his Leaving Certificate. She was so proud. She had done a good job, and the neighbours all commended her. She could feel the pride well up inside her. His aunts and uncles and cousins were always there, and of course his grandparents all beaming and smiling with pride and love. He had a bright future ahead of him until it all changed.

Caught in a web of youthful recklessness, drink and drugs, it all fell apart. The next family gathering was on the steps of the Four Courts. More photographs without the cousins, aunts and uncles, photographs his mother avoids looking at.

Imprisoned On The Outside: Free On The Inside

THE OFFICER opened the door and pointed to the bottom bunk. The top one was already spoken for: first in got the top bunk and the remote control. He didn't care. He was home! He didn't want to be out there. He doesn't belong out there anymore, and he hopes the judge will give him a lengthy sentence for the three robberies he committed out there.

'I thrive in prison,' he explains to the chaplain. 'I am locked up on the outside and free on the inside.' He was first confined in a state institution when he was eight years old. As a child, he was detained, and as a teenager imprisoned. Thirty-two years later, he is still in a system not designed to care for the outcast and the delinquent but to keep them out of sight.

This Is How I Cope

HE ASSURES the chaplain that he does not need to attend the Bereavement Support Group. He is in too much pain to listen to other people's grief. He just wants to write the names of his deceased family members in nice print and have it framed – the names of his parents, his brothers and sisters and the most loved of all, his granny. He will never forget his granny and comes to Mass every Sunday just to remember her. And when he is out he will he will visit her grave. That is all that is left of her. That is his way of coping. He does not want to talk about his losses with others or share his grief. No, he will just keep them all in the framed picture of his memory.

Silent Emotionless Grief

HE HAS just been told by the prison chaplain that his mother is seriously ill and may die. He shows no emotion. He just stares into space. The unravelling of his story is a slow, painful process as he struggles with memories of childhood abuse, addiction and broken relationships.

He and his siblings had been taken into care at an early age. He is now *in care* again – in the care of the state. Care? A strange word that. He had never really experienced care and is not too sure what it means. I wonder did the judge care when he sentenced him to prison. But, how was the judge to know his story – the long story that wasn't care, that isn't care?

He shows no emotion. Years of being in care have taught him not to care. Years of burying emotions have helped him to survive. It is how you survive in prison too. It is the only way. This is how he will cope with his mother's death.

Does he grieve? Is he able to grieve? Is he able to grieve for the lost years of childhood, for the lost years of doing time? Will he be able to grieve for his lost mother?

As he shuts his cell door, he shuts out the flooding emotions of pain, loss and grief. Nobody will notice.

Nothing Nobody Nowhere

HE IS sixty-two and has spent most of those sixty-two years in state institutions or prison. He now lives in a Dublin Hostel. One of his earliest memories is of being taken by his mother to what he describes as a 'big house'. He has no idea what age he was at the time.

When he was eighteen, having spent a number of years in various religious and state institutions, he decided to go in search of his mother. He had no address, just the name. In spite of this scant information he discovered where his mother lived and went to meet her.

His most vivid memory of the day is of a basin in the corner of the room catching the falling rain as it came through the roof. He and his mother chatted awkwardly for a short while, and then she told him not to come again. She would, however, meet him when doing her weekly shopping in the market.

The meetings continued for a while and sometimes his mother gave him a ten shilling note. Communication between them was at best awkward, and he stopped going to the market on Saturday mornings. Something had changed within him. Memories. Two years later he returned to the house. She was no longer there. She was dead. So too was he.

There was now nobody, nowhere to go, nothing.

Where Is He Now?

I WONDER where he is now, the young prisoner who was too frightened to speak. I had never witnessed such fear before. 'Because of his fear he refused to speak to me,' the inspector said. He went on to say, 'This is the first time that any prisoner, in any prison, had displayed such fear in my presence.'

In the vision statement of the Irish Prison Service we read about safety, security and humane treatment. But, how humane is it when you are silenced and paralysed by fear?

But, where is he now?

Is he still frightened, too frightened to speak, or has he learned the prisoner's way of coping? How to cope with fear, with violence, with bullying. Did he ever tell anyone why he couldn't or wouldn't speak? Maybe not. It's not manly to be fearful. Does anyone know where he is now? Why was he there anyway? Why was he locked up at such an early age? What had he done to deserve this? What have we as a society done or failed to do? What have I done or failed to do?

The Babe In The Womb

IT IS Holy Week. She is visiting him for the last time before giving birth to their third child. The baby will be delivered by caesarean section the following day. One can only imagine the conversation that might take place between them. He is on a drug-free landing in the prison and he has never taken drugs. Because of his good behavior, he enjoys trustee status. She has been visiting him regularly since his incarceration. The visits were difficult for her, but worth it just to see him. They were difficult for him too.

Today is just another visit but more difficult under the circumstances. All is well until she is paraded in front of the sniffer dog. The dog sits, thereby indicating that she may be carrying drugs. No account is taken of the fact that he does not take drugs, is on a drug-free landing and works as a trustee. No account is taken of the fact that she is heavily pregnant and about to give birth. She is offered a screen visit. She cries throughout the visit as she looks through a screen at the father of her unborn child.

I am reminded of John the Baptist, who when visited by the pregnant Mary leaps in his mother's womb. He leaps for joy! I wonder about that other pregnant woman and the baby in her womb. The unborn curled in the womb feeling the stress, the humiliation and the desperation of its parents.

When Did I See You In Prison And Not Visit You?

HE IS twenty-three, and he is in prison. Nobody visits him. There are no names on his phone card. There is nobody to phone. He is on twenty-three-hour lockup for his own protection. He got a hiding shortly after coming in. It was terrifying, and he fears a repeat. He froze when the door opened to allow the chaplain in, and her assurances that he was safe while she was there did little to relax him. It is his first prison sentence. How is he to know that you are always safe while the chaplain is around? All he knows is fear. Fear emanates from his very eyes. Fear wrecks his small slender frame. Fear reduces his voice to an almost inaudible whisper.

The chaplain explains that she has spoken to his mother. She is ok but not ready to talk to him yet. He feels a surge of anger towards her. What if he doesn't want to talk to her when she is ready?

He talks to the chaplain. There is nobody else. He asks her to try to make contact with one of his friends. She tries and fails. The phone number is no longer in use.

At What Time Did She Die?

HE IS slowly moving away from his family. He makes fewer phone calls now and limits his family visits. After eighteen years it is easier this way. But the deep connection with his family is strong. It is an unbroken and unquenchable connection that binds us to kith and kin no matter the time or distance that divide us. Today, he senses something is wrong. He is agitated and unable to settle. Night falls and day dawns. Towards evening of that same day, he notices the chaplain come towards his door. He moves back into the cell knowing why she is coming. Who is it, is it my niece? he asks nervously. The chaplain, taken aback, nods her head.

They begin to talk and the story of his niece begins to unravel. He remembers the day she was born to his unmarried sister. The sister who brought shame on the family by her behaviour. But somehow the baby made all things well, and as she grew bigger and began to smile and do all the things babies do, so too did the household begin to smile and let shine from their very soul the deep love they had for her within their hearts. She spread happiness and they responded with love.

His only question was 'At what time did she die?' The chaplain told him. It was the time he had felt the deep unease within.

Rest In Peace

HE HAS been in and out of prison since he was a nipper. In the beginning he came in to visit his Da. He always looked forward to the visits but always came away feeling sad. The sight of his Da being taken away and his Ma pulling him after her as he kept looking back still haunts him. 'Come on', his mother would say as she steered him through the doors and gates of the prison. He never understood why she was in such a hurry. He loved his Da.

He is now the one being visited. His Da never comes. He never did. But, his Ma? 'Ah well, your Ma is different.' She visited him in every prison in the land and beyond. He spent time in Her Majesty's prisons too. Her recent letter is disturbing to him. She will not be coming in again. She is no longer able. Even more disturbing is his mother's last line. 'I will never rest until you are free.' Never rest in peace.

They Won't Know Who They Are

A SMALL group of teenagers gather to meet the special guest. They are not too sure who she is but they know she is someone important. Some remain silent or giddy, not too sure what to do. A spokesperson emerges. He grasps the situation and speaks for the others. He points to two of his companions who have been sentenced to unusually long sentences and prophetically says: 'By the time they get out, they won't know who they are.'

These few prophetic words spoken by the teenage prisoner sum up the reality of the effects of imprisonment. Out of the mouth of babes. It was true for the two teenagers that morning and equally true for all we confine to imprisonment. And the longer we hold them, the worse it will be for them. The indelible mark of imprisonment remains imprinted in the depth of their being.

This Is Where
I Feel At Home

HE HAS returned to prison. His brief sojourn on the outside has abruptly ended. He was glad. He couldn't hack it out there. His head was melted. His head was wrecked. His head was all over the place. He was glad the guards arrested him, and when the prison officer opened the cell door and pointed to his bunk, he felt at home again. He hoped the judge would give him a long sentence. He can't cope on the outside.

He will await sentence, innocent until proven guilty, in the no man's land of a remand prison; where walking a prison yard is part of a daily routine.

Is this better than what we can offer him on the outside? Does anyone care that a young twenty-five-year-old man will aimlessly walk the prison yard rather than the streets of his home town?

May You See Your Children's Children

'THIS IS no place for sadness' – poignant words from the young man lying on his hard, thin mattress in the darkened cell. He has been refused permission to attend the funeral of his cousin. They were reared together like brother and sister by their Granny, a common feature in the life of this generation of grannies who have been called upon to rear their children's children.

The authorities say that as she is his cousin, and not his sister, he can't be allowed to attend the funeral or even view the remains and say his goodbye. It is his first experience of the death of someone close to him. He struggles to believe she is dead. Maybe it is a mistake. Disbelief turns to anger. What was she up to? If I had been around this would not have happened. Grief, anger and despair all combine to heighten his anguish and frustration in his darkened cell.

His friends are fearful and leave him alone. He needs to be alone until he can bravely emerge from the darkness of his inner being with the mask of the hardened man, to mingle again with his fear-filled colleagues.

I Was Sick And You Visited Me

HE LIES handcuffed in the hospital bed. He understands why, but his mother doesn't. Her heart aches. She would love to hug him but feels awkward. He understands. He is embarrassed and ashamed in front of his mother and feels for her. She has brought his little sister. He loves his little sister. Maybe she won't notice the handcuffs. She does and is afraid. She says nothing, just stands and stares. She will ask her mother when they get outside, maybe, or maybe not. Her mother always gets upset – annoyed and angry – when they visit him. His sister has learned to say nothing until her mother is herself again. She senses her mother's ache and her brother's awkwardness, but doesn't know what to do. She feels fear and is frightened.

The combined and unspoken feelings of mother and son intermingle, and the emotional distance deepens. The hurried goodbyes bring little relief.

She May Be Dead

HE STANDS at the gate waiting to see the chaplain. It is quiet on the drag now, and he will be able to have a word with her on his own. Nobody will notice. Maybe she will be able to help. He came into prison last week and nobody knows where he is, not that this will matter too much to anybody, still.

He has no phone numbers or can't remember any. The last he heard of his mother she was in a nursing home. She had lost her memory and didn't remember him. He wonders if she is still alive. She may be dead by now. The thought scares him but he needs to know.

He stands looking left and right. Nobody notices him. Nobody knows him. Yeah, they know his name and prison number, he was here before. He has a name and a number. That is who he is. He has no address, no family contacts, just a few so-called friends and that is all. And his mother? Even if she didn't remember him she was still there. He had her.

The chaplain eventually arrives doing her rounds. She remembers him from before, and he is pleased. It is nice to be remembered! And she knows his name. They try to piece together the scant information he has about his mother. She will ring around and hopefully find where she is or was. He is scared.

Life After Prison?

HE HAD been out of prison for almost six years. He did well on the inside and emerged with a place in a third-level educational institution. We had high hopes for him and felt proud that we had played some small part in his success. He too had high hopes. He had secured accommodation and was afforded an opportunity to attend therapy. All was good, so good in fact that he was invited to speak at a conference and was interviewed by the media at the event.

As time passed, however, the weight of his past began to overwhelm him, and his confidence eroded. Relationships became more and more difficult, even within his family circle. They had supported him while in prison but now wished to free themselves from him. The slow realisation of oncoming isolation and rejection played into his already weakened confidence. Self-isolation and rejection added to the burden. He dropped out of college, changed his accommodation and tried to create a new identity for himself.

Life improved and he met a new girlfriend. All was well until her family learned of his past. Another ending, another beginning for him. How many more beginnings and endings would he have to make? Is there life after prison?

Forget

HE IS twenty years old. His father has died, and his sister has come to the prison to tell him. There is only the two of them, and their relationship is strained and fractured. Their grief is cloaked in awkwardness and emotionless dialogue. The one remaining link between them gone, they now face a divided and lonely future.

Back in his cell, he bangs out his door and tries to come to grips with his grief, guilt and regret. Why? What if? What's the point? All is lost. All is gone forever. Prison is his refuge for now and then homelessness and the streets.

Memories of his mother come flooding back. The pain and torment he inflicted on her and her unfailing love and forgiveness all come to haunt him in his isolation and despair. Is there any glimmer of light for him? Any glimmer of hope?

Morning will come and he will rise to another day on the inside. He will keep the mask of manliness on before the others. No need for anyone to know his father has died, and it will be easier for him to forget.

Endless Waiting

HE IS waiting. Waiting to see if he will be given permission to attend his brother's funeral. His brother has died. The waiting is punctuated by bouts of anger and repressed grief. His whole energy is focused on *getting out.*

At this point nothing else matters, even his brother's death. His desire and real need to be with family blots out all else. Time is passing. Arrangements are being made and his family is waiting too.

He waits. They wait. Wait to hear whether a brother can be given time out to bury his brother. No answer is given. Night passes behind locked doors. Waiting. No answer comes next morning. The waiting is over when his brother is buried without him.

It is then the repressed anger takes hold, and even the small kindnesses offered to him, the extra phone call, the family room visit, the promise of a visit to his brother's grave at a later date merely serve to further anger him. Nothing will ever compensate for not being allowed attend his brother's funeral.

Alone

HE SMOKES almost non-stop. He is considered a risk to himself and to others, and often finds himself on lockup. He finds it difficult to relate to others and many of his *companions* on his landing just ignore him. He is a tragic figure, a lonely figure. He constantly looks for a bit of dust, a cigarette lighter or a few skins. But, most of all he craves a little attention. His small, emaciated figure goes almost unnoticed on the crowded landing. His small, emaciated figure carries the depth of an unknown and unarticulated story. It is a story that may never be told.

Family relationships were difficult and are now non-existent. They are unable to cope with the pain his actions visited on them, and fail to appreciate his suffering and his longing for their support. He is alone in his misery.

Abused And Abuser

HE IS an elderly man. Prison is no problem to him. He has served time over and over, again and again. But this time it is different. It is different for two reasons. Recently he disclosed to the chaplain that he had been abused by a priest many years ago. He had not reported it before and was not sure why he is reporting it now. Strange how things happen to him. A bit like his crimes. He never sets out to commit crime but somehow he does. He doesn't expect anyone to believe this but somehow it is true. At this stage he hardly believes it himself, *but* it must be true. He is consumed by guilt and longs for some peace. There is no peace.

The Church's counselling service, established to help survivors of abuse, is of little help to him in his present turmoil. But maybe it will help. He's not sure. The raking up of old wounds and pain leaves him feeling vulnerable and disturbed. Coming back to a prison cell following a deep intimate disclosure of past abuse and humiliation is hardly conducive to healing. He's not sure he wants to continue. But maybe he should. Maybe it will eventually help. It is not helping him now.

The abuse, he says, is no excuse for his crimes. He makes no connection. The guilt is eating into him and destroying him. He is the abused and the abuser.

The prison authorities take little notice of him these days. He is no longer a risk to the security of the state or the smooth running of one of its penal institutions. He is tired, tired of prison, tired of criminal activities, tired of life. Just tired. His energies are slowly eroding with guilt, age and despair. There is no peace.

Do This In Memory Of Me

WE GATHER around the small four-by-four table having already placed a small white cloth, a candle, the bread and wine, and the small drop of water to cleanse the chalice on it. This is our setting for Sunday Mass with the seventeen-year-old children in the prison. There is a hundred per cent attendance for our weekly celebration of the Eucharist. We sit around the table under the watchful eyes of prison officers.

This is special. It is simple with none of the ornate trimmings of liturgical celebrations. The homily focuses on the Word of God in the light of seventeen-year-olds. They listen, ask questions and sometimes just switch off!

Holy Thursday Night

THE SOLEMNITY is not fully appreciated by the small congregation gathered for the washing of the feet and the celebration of the Last Supper. Yet there is something special about Holy Thursday night in a prison.

In a state of drugged consciousness, he wanders in talking to himself and to anyone else who will listen to him. His aunt has died and this is his way of coping. There is no trouble in getting volunteers to have their feet washed. 'It's a holy thing to do,' one fellow says as he encourages others to join him.

Necks are strained to observe the ritual. And so 'the great act of love' is recreated and re-enacted. I wonder what it was like in that upper room of Jerusalem. But, this is our upper room where we wash or have our feet washed. We wash each other's feet in the daily grind of imprisonment, in the waters of separation and isolation, in the weariness of doing time, endless time. We just wash each other's feet.

This is an upper room never depicted by artist or craftsman. This is our upper room where he who washed feet is still washing feet, the feet of his loved ones with no less love and care than on that first Holy Thursday Night. 'Lord, not my feet only but also my hands and my head!' (Jn 13:9).

And as the prisoner returns to his cell, he is accompanied by the great Feet Washer who spent His night in prison awaiting His trial.

Pope Francis is often pictured washing the feet of women or prisoners, with some pious inscriptions written underneath. No such pictures or pious inscriptions will ever issue from our prison, but the washing of the feet is no less significant.

Silent Night, Holy Night

IT IS Christmas night. The prison is locked down. Night staff cover the prison wings. All is silent; all is quiet. Silent Night, Holy Night. Silently locked away in prison cells and prison beds, lie the imprisoned. Imprisoned in the cell of their very being on this Christmas night. Silent Night, Holy Night.

Locked safely away, not in the warmness of a stable or crib, but in the coldness of a prison cell. Condemned to a life that is no life, as the world celebrates the coming of Life. There is no room in the inn of life tonight for the imprisoned.

The locked-down prison contains the silence within its harsh walls, but not the loud unheard noise in the locked minds and hearts of its imprisoned. Blocked out memories cry out for release. There is no release. The pounding head noises resound against the uncaring walls, but go unheard, encaged forever within condemned heads.

It will soon be morning and another Christmas will be over.

The Letter

HE IS standing by the bunk bed reading a letter in the semi-darkness. It's a short one and from his mother. She never used to write to him, she always came to visit. However, she won't be coming again. It is not that she doesn't want to, she is not able anymore.

He puts the letter aside. Memories come flooding back: every prison he was in, his mother always came to visit. She never let him down. The letter lies on his bunk bed. He won't read it again.

Life has changed forever. The one constant in his life is gone forever. She is not dead, but she is gone, gone forever from his life; a life she never understood but always loved. A life she brought into the world in pain and joy, a life she lost, tried to find but failed. Broken by the hardships of life, the constant yearning for the soul of her son and the weariness of old age, she wrote the letter.

The Court Room

THE PARENTS sit in the court room side by side. They listen to the arguments from the defence and from the prosecution. Is this the son they had reared and loved; the one they nurtured and guided through all the years? What had happened to him? Where did he or they go wrong? He is slowly slipping from them and there is nothing they can do. They try not to listen. The voices keep pounding in their wearied heads. This is worse than a death. It is a death; they have lost him.

The Unanswered Letter

HE LIES in the bottom bunk bed facing the wall of his cell, in a foetal-like position. There is no relief now and never will be.

He has just received the news of his father's death, the one person he needs to be reconciled with. Over many years he had written and torn up numerous letters, begging his father's forgiveness. No letter ever succeeded in giving expression to his feelings of guilt and remorse. Eventually, he sent a letter and waited for the reply. It never came.

But, there was always hope that someday the letter would come. Now he knew it never would. Nothing mattered anymore.

This Is It

THE GATES open and close. The van moves into an enclosed space and stops. Doors are opened and closed, and he hears muffled voices. It makes no difference what is happening, or what they are saying. He has arrived at his destination. This is it. He has crossed the threshold for life. Too numb to feel frightened. This is it. The van starts up again. The door behind closes and another opens onto a yard.

He has arrived. Handcuffed, he is taken inside and then to reception, the arrivals area. He sees no sign of a departures area. Tomorrow will come and many more tomorrows.

I Became Somebody

HE WAS transferred from another prison as an elderly man. Having spent many years in prison, he was used to the system and just fitted in. He knew what to do and had no great expectations of life. He came from a large family, but only one brother had kept in touch after all this time. His mother was in a nursing home and he hadn't seen her for years. He still loved her and would love to see her again, not that there was much chance of that happening. He was resigned.

He had just one request. In primary school he was in the remedial class. He remembered his teacher and had fond memories of her. She also taught in the local girls' school and this involved moving from one school to the other every day. She had books and bits and pieces to carry, and she always asked him to help her. A big smile would break out on his face every time he mentioned her and recounted the story of carrying her books and her bits and pieces. This was his job.

But, where was she now?

The search began and she was found. She remembered him too and so began a new beginning in his life. She visited him over and over again. He felt important again just like he used to when he carried her books and her bits and pieces from one school to the other.

CONCLUSION

THE ADVENT of Covid-19 brought the curtain down on my time in the prison. There were no goodbyes. It just happened. I was one of the people told to cocoon, and I reluctantly obeyed orders. But, in reality the time had come. It was time to go. Life had been good to me. The years I had spent among the imprisoned, and the people I worked with along the way, were precious. There were probably the best years I had ever known, and I am grateful for them. The words of St Paul to the Philippians – 'I thank my God each time I think of you and when I pray for you I pray with joy' (Phil 1:3–4) – sum up my feelings at this time, and while no longer physically present in the prison, my heart is still there and always will be.

I am now devoting whatever time is left to me to working with the families of people in prison and making up for when, as chaplain, I didn't have enough time to devote to them. The families are very often the forgotten ones, and their pain and suffering can go unrecognised. What I witnessed on a daily basis in the prison was the sheer goodness, loyalty and support of family members visiting the prison week after week, sometimes for many years. They just kept coming, silently reflecting an unconditional love that can only come from a deep inner goodness. No sermon or homily could ever adequately give expression to what unconditional love is. It must be witnessed, and it was my privilege to witness it being lived out within prison walls.

The families too are hidden voices and must be invited to the table when the conversation begins. They carry the untold stories of fathers and mothers, who though innocent of any wrongdoing, carry an undeserved guilt and shame. I witnessed deep silences in visiting waiting rooms, people sitting apart, each carrying their own unspoken sadness and unanswered questions.

I don't have the answers, but once the conversation begins the answers will emerge, because the experts, namely those who have first-hand experience, will help us understand. The myriad voices will create a cacophony releasing as yet unheard truths that will free us to move into new and creative ways of restoring right relationships in our communities and among our people. The criminal justice system will emerge from being adversarial and punitive to being restorative and healing. Society will experience a new transformation. Its weakest members will be given a place at the table of life with their sisters and brothers.